Thanks, Again!

More Simple, Inexpensive Ways for Busy Leaders to Recognize Staff

Nelson Scott

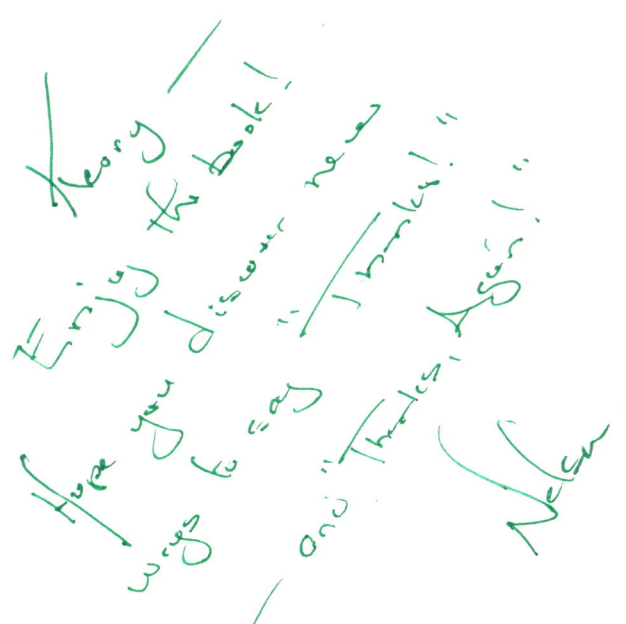

 FriesenPress

One Printers Way
Altona, MB R0G 0B0
Canada

www.friesenpress.com

Copyright © 2023 by Nelson Scott
First Edition — 2023

All rights reserved.

No part of this publication may be reproduced in any form, or by any means, electronic or mechanical, including photocopying, recording, or any information browsing, storage, or retrieval system, without permission in writing from FriesenPress.

ISBN
978-1-03-916801-5 (Hardcover)
978-1-03-916800-8 (Paperback)
978-1-03-916802-2 (eBook)

1. BUSINESS & ECONOMICS, HUMAN RESOURCES & PERSONNEL MANAGEMENT

Distributed to the trade by The Ingram Book Company

This book was conceived and created in *amiskwacîwâskahikan* (Edmonton) on Treaty 6 territory, the traditional meeting grounds, gathering place and travelling route for the Cree, Saulteaux, Blackfoot, Métis, Denė and Nakota Sioux. We are all treaty people.

In Memory of my Parents

H. Bruce Scott, 1912-1957
Thelma J. Scott, 1913-2016

I miss you both.

Table of Contents

Tip #1 xi
   The 4 As of Staff Recognition

**First, a Bit About You,
the Reader** xiii

Section I
Laying the Foundation 1

Theme #1 3
   Recognition Builds
   Workplace Relationships
   What is "Staff Recognition?". . .6

Theme #2 8
   Filling Your Staff Recognition
   Tool Kit

Theme #3 12
   GREAT Staff Recognition:
   5 Pieces that Make the
   Picture of Appreciation and
   Gratitude Complete
   Genuine: Ensuring Staff
   Recognition is Authentic. 13
   Relevant: Making Staff
   Recognition Strategic 15

   Explicit: Making Staff
   Recognition Specific 19
   Appropriate: Personalizing Staff
   Recognition 22
   Timely: Putting Staff Recognition
   in the Moment 26

Theme #4 29
   Senior Executives, Frontline Staff
   and Recognition

Theme #5 33
   Making Staff Recognition a Habit

Section II. 37
Using Your Staff Recognition Tools

Theme #6 39
   Staff Recognition's Number One
   Tool: Thank-You Notes

Theme #7 42
   Recognition That Sticks

Theme #8 45
   Building Commitment from
   Day One

Theme #9 53
Discovering the Most Appropriate Ways to Recognize Staff
7 Questions to Ask to Recognize Staff Appropriately 57

Theme #10 59
Linking Staff Recognition to Career Goals

Theme #11 64
Mine Customer Feedback for Reasons to Recognize Staff

Theme #12 68
Vacation-Themed Staff Recognition

Theme #13 71
Include Family Members in Your Staff Recognition Plans

Theme #14 75
Important? Certainly. But Recognition Can Be Fun, Too

Theme #15 82
A Year's Worth of Staff Recognition
Springtime, when Recognition Blossoms................84
Recognition for a Summer's Day....................87
Let Recognition Fall Like Autumn Leaves...........89
Recognition that Removes Winter's Chill.............91

Theme #16 95
Add Meaning to Formal Recognition

Theme 17 99
The Gift of Time

Theme #18 102
Staff Recognition Goes Green

Theme #19 104
Assessing Your Staff Recognition Practices
Surveys: How to Ask.......108

Section III 111
Responding to Staff Recognition Needs of Specific Groups

Theme #20 113
Recognition by Everyone: Unleashing the Power of Peer Recognition
Part A: How Leaders Can Encourage Peer Recognition .114
Part B: How Staff Members Can Recognize Their Peers 118

Theme #21 121
Recognition of Staff Who Work Remotely

Theme #22 126
Diverse and Inclusive: Recognition for Workplaces Where All Feel They Belong

Theme #23 134
Recognize Bosses on Their Day—and All Year Long

Theme #24 138
Team Recognition

Section IV 143
Overcoming Barriers to Recognition

Theme #25 145
A Penny-Pincher's Guide to Staff Recognition

Theme #26 148
Staff Recognition Time Savers

Theme #27 150
How to Respond the Next Time Someone Says, "I Don't Recognize Staff Because . . ."

Theme #28 153
Practices to Avoid When Recognizing Staff

Theme #29 157
A Verbal Eraser and Other Words that are Barriers to Staff Recognition

Theme #30 159
Avoiding the "Participation Ribbon" Trap

Bonus Section 163
At Least 101 More Staff Recognition Thoughts, Tips, Tools and Techniques

A Final Request........... 188
Become a Staff Recognition Evangelist!

Notes.................. 189

Acknowledgements......... 193

Conversation Starters for Book Clubs and Staff Recognition Mastermind Groups 195

Want more Nelson?......... 200

Tip #1
The 4 As of Staff Recognition

Not all staff recognition tips are created equally. Some will work for you. Others won't. Some can be modified to fit your circumstances.

Use the following to assess the tips, tools and techniques you will encounter in this book and elsewhere:

Adopt recognition tips with which you are comfortable and which you feel will fit your workplace culture.

Adapt others so they fit your circumstances. Let these tips inspire you to discover new ways to recognize staff.

Avoid those staff recognition practices with which you are uncomfortable or which you feel won't align with your workplace culture.

Abandon staff recognition practices that don't work or have become stale.

First, a Bit About You, the Reader

The most frequent reaction to me telling someone that I write and speak about staff recognition is, "That's really needed. I know someone (often their current or former boss) who needs to hear your message."

They continue to describe how recognition is a rare commodity where they work or where they once worked. They feel they are not now, or were not previously, valued or appreciated.

Realistically, their managers and supervisors are not the audience for this book. Of course, those individuals should learn about staff recognition, but those who are unable to fathom the benefits of expressing appreciation in the workplace are unlikely to purchase a book filled with staff recognition tips.

> Greek philosopher Aristotle is credited with the observation that "nature abhors a vacuum." The same is true in the workplace in the absence of feedback of any kind. Eliminate feedback vacuums by providing negative feedback when required and recognition when deserved. The absence of recognition and words of encouragement creates a vacuum that staff will soon fill with negative thoughts. They will assume that the boss is unhappy with their performance but reluctant to deliver bad news. Without praise for what they do well, they will begin to worry about what they have done wrong.

They will continue to "lead" workplaces characterized by poor morale, low engagement and high turnover, and wonder why.

But that's not your workplace.

This book is for frontline leaders like you—managers, supervisors, school principals, small business owners, department heads and others who grasp the power of staff recognition.[1]

You are a *believer*! You understand that acknowledging the contributions and achievements of individual staff members and teams makes a difference. You don't need to be convinced that you should express appreciation frequently.

Believing in the power of recognition means you stand out from most managers and supervisors. Research by Gallup and Workhuman found that four of every five leaders said staff recognition was not a priority for them, and roughly two thirds said they had no budget for staff recognition.

That's why I've devoted little space to arguing the benefits of staff recognition, apart from sprinkled references to a few studies that confirm what you already believe. If you are looking for more evidence, check out my first book (*Thanks! GREAT Job!*[2]), review the counter arguments to the reasons some managers give for not recognizing staff in Theme #27: How to Respond the Next Time Someone Says, "I Don't Recognize Staff Because . . ." (p. 150), read any of the fine books by others listed in Theme #2: Filling Your Staff Recognition Tool Kit (p. 8), or just Google, "Why is staff recognition important?"

Despite your history of success in recognizing staff, you are likely still looking for new ways to say thank you in your workplace. There is always a place for new staff recognition practices. In this book, you will find tools and techniques you can use immediately and others that are the spark that ignites your imagination to develop your own unique recognition practices.

Because most frontline leaders have limited resources (specifically, little time or money) to devote to staff recognition, most of the tools, tips and

---

1 While written primarily with frontline leaders in mind, senior leaders and frontline staff could also find the content of interest. In particular, Theme #5: Senior Executives, Frontline Staff and Recognition (p. 29) is meant for senior leaders, while Theme #20: Recognition by Everyone: Unleashing the Power of Peer Recognition, Part B (p. 118) and Theme #23: Recognize Bosses on Their Day—and All Year Long (p. 134) will be of value for frontline staff.

2 Available from www.GREATstaffrecognition.com

techniques in this book are inexpensive and easy to implement. These are "low-cost, high-value" ways to strengthen your expressions of gratitude—low cost in terms of your time, effort and money and high value as perceived by recipients.

As you browse this collection of ways to recognize staff, highlight those that you could use, mark those that will need to be changed to fit your workplace and cross out those which are simply not right for you.

The book is organized by themes, each one including a brief introduction, followed by related staff recognition tips, tools and techniques.

The themes are divided into four sections—Laying the Foundation, Using Your Staff Recognition Tools, Responding to Staff Recognition Needs of Specific Groups and Overcoming Barriers to Staff Recognition. There is also a bonus section with ideas that didn't fit any of the themes but were too good to leave out.

Finally, like a murder mystery, there is a reveal at the end of the book. But unlike a whodunit, it's OK to turn to the last page to discover who *will do it*.

Section I
Laying the Foundation

Defining staff recognition and why it's important; creating your staff recognition tool kit; the staff recognition role of senior executives; making a habit of recognizing staff.

Theme #1
Recognition Builds Workplace Relationships

An audience member in one of my programs once observed that recognition is all about building relationships. How true!

Staff members' experience with the boss is the most important relationship in the workplace. When frontline leaders care about their staff, are fair in their dealings with them and treat them with respect, it creates a work environment where staff feel they belong. Staff members are willing to do their best *for the boss* and are less likely to leave.

Feeling they are valued as individuals and appreciated for how they contribute and for what they achieve makes staff members more confident about how they do their jobs. Well-delivered recognition creates an emotional connection between frontline leaders and staff members and among co-workers. It connects them to their work and to the organization and its purpose, which can increase employee happiness and engagement and improve retention.

> **Why Recognize Staff?**
> - Staff members want and deserve to know they are valued as individuals and appreciated for how they contribute and what they achieve.
> - There is a benefit for you: It feels good to acknowledge others for performing well.

Your messages of appreciation may be the boost recipients need to lift their performance from good to great.

Recognition creates workplaces where staff members believe they are right where they belong and feel comfortable being themselves. It's where they want to stay. "The best teams care for and support one another," writes former National Hockey League player Mark Messier in his memoir, *No One Wins Alone*. "They have to. Who's going to give his all, or function at his best, if he doesn't feel like he belongs?"

Recognition does not exist in isolation. Recognition thrives in a culture of appreciation, trust and respect. How you recognize staff must be congruent with the workplace culture, including its values and mission statement.

When Michael Burchell and Jennifer Robin, authors of *The Great Workplace*, asked, "Is your organization a great place to work?" and "Why?" what they heard from staff members who felt theirs was a great workplace was that "they believe their leaders to be credible, respectful and fair—they trust them."

Recognition increases the level of trust. Research shows that 90 per cent of staff members who receive recognition trust the boss who provides that recognition, while only 48 per cent of those who do not receive recognition feel the same. When staff members trust you and their colleagues, they will feel comfortable coming forward with their concerns and questions.

> **How Frequently Should You Recognize Staff?**
>
> Recent research found that 42 per cent of Millennials (a.k.a. Generation Y, born 1981-1996) expected to receive feedback weekly. What about older workers? The study revealed that fewer of them have this expectation, but it's likely they would also like to receive frequent feedback, particularly if it is positive or at least delivered in a positive and helpful manner.

Without respect and trust, attempts at recognition will be regarded as empty rituals rather than **Genuine** expressions of appreciation for what people achieve and how they contribute.

The risk of a book like this, filled with suggestions on how to recognize staff, is that readers may conclude that thank-you notes, gift cards, trinkets and other gestures of appreciation are necessary elements of recognition that recipients will value. They aren't.

The tips, tools and techniques in this book are simply *aids* to convey messages of appreciation to staff, co-workers and even bosses.

Words matter. In particular, your words matter. They matter to the people with whom you work. Words of appreciation make a difference in your workplace. Your words convey how you feel about what staff members do more effectively than any token or gesture.

While the right items, carefully selected with the recipient in mind, can strengthen your message of appreciation, they are simply vehicles to help convey your message. They are only effective when used by individuals inspired by a **Genuine** sense of appreciation for what staff members did. Any tokens of appreciation should be accompanied by a specific description of how the recipient contributed or what was achieved and why it was important.

In the words of 17th century French dramatist Pierre Corneille, "The manner of giving is worth more than the gifts."

Tokens and gestures of appreciation are the exclamation marks of staff recognition. They highlight your words. They underline them and make them stand out.

Selecting the **Appropriate** way to recognize staff elevates the value of recognition in the recipient's mind.

> **A Final Thought**
> You never know what impact your small gesture of gratitude will have on the lives of staff members. Your words could be exactly what they need to hear. Express gratitude frequently.

What is "Staff Recognition?"

Recognition:
1. The art of recognizing someone or something
2. The state of being recognized
3. The perception or acknowledgment of something as true or valid
4. Appreciation of achievement, merit, services, etc., or an expression of this
5. Formal acknowledgment conveying approval

– Random House College Dictionary

***

"Employee recognition is a key element of a successful business strategy that focuses on acknowledging and celebrating employee achievements. Organizations develop recognition strategies to motivate employees and reinforce desired behaviors."

– Recognition Professionals International
https://www.recognition.org

***

"Recognition is defined as seeing and acknowledging an employee and their value."

– Cindy Ventrice
Make Their Day! Employee Recognition that Works

***

"To acknowledge and appreciate those behaviors, practices and actions that move us toward achieving our business goals and objectives and that establish a working environment that promotes the values and concepts of loyalty, belonging, confidence, self-worth, teamwork, respect, creativity and trust through frequent and sincere methods of approval."

– Sue Glasscock and Kimberly Gram
Workplace Recognition: Step-by-step examples of a positive reinforcement strategy

What is "Staff Recognition?"

***

"Recognition comes from the heart: Compensation is what you give people for doing the job they were hired to do. Recognition is something you give when people do more than what's expected of them. Effective recognition must come from the heart."

– David Rye
Attracting and Rewarding Outstanding Employees

***

"Recognition is a positive consequence provided to a person for a behavior or result. Recognition can take the form of acknowledgment, approval, or the expression of gratitude. It means appreciating someone for something he or she has done for you, your group, or your organization. You can give recognition as someone strives to achieve a certain goal or behavior or upon completion of that goal or behavior. Using recognition, organizations can build engagement and drive success for the company, including all stakeholders."

– Bob Nelson
Recognizing & Engaging Employees for Dummies

"Recognition is about noticing the small-scale wins that lead to meaningful progress and showing employees you care about them and their success."

– Achievers

Theme #2
Filling Your Staff Recognition Tool Kit

"Give us the tools and we will finish the job."

– Sir Winston Churchill

Prepare to recognize staff by creating your own staff recognition tool kit, filled with tips and what you need to deliver recognition:

Include these tools in your staff recognition tool kit and keep them close at hand so that you can recognize the contributions of staff members when opportunities arise:

- Thank-you and other cards (congratulations, birthday, blank, etc.)
- A pen with an ink colour reserved only for recognition
- Sticky notes of assorted colours and shapes
- Treats that staff members enjoy
- Fun coupons for an extended break or the opportunity to leave early or come in late
- Small gifts
- Coffee shop and other gift cards, movie passes, etc. (If your budget permits)

***

Thanks, Again! or another collection of staff recognition tips also has a place in your staff recognition kit. Go through and highlight those tips that resonate with you—those that will work for you and in your organization. Mark others as techniques that you could adapt to fit the culture of your workplace. Cross out those to avoid because they aren't right for you, your staff or your workplace.

These books are a rich source of staff recognition tips: *1,501 Ways to Reward Employees* by Bob Nelson; *The 1001 Rewards and Recognition Fieldbook* by Bob Nelson and Dean Spitzer; *The Carrot Principle* or *Managing with Carrots* by Adrian Gostick and Chester Elton; *Make Their Day!* by Cindy Ventrice; and *Thanks! GREAT Job!* by Nelson Scott.

***

Ask acquaintances and leaders from other organizations how they recognize staff. What works for them may work for you. Some practices will need to be modified to fit the culture of your workplace and others may just not fit the culture of your workplace. There may be some techniques that don't work for them that could work for you. Your different approach and delivery may change what was ineffective for others into tools which you can use to provide meaningful recognition.

***

Keep a "Future Recognition Journal," filled with tools and techniques you might use to recognize staff in the future. Add to the list as you learn how other people recognize staff.

***

Establish a staff recognition mastermind group by bringing together other managers and supervisors who share your commitment to recognizing staff, so you can learn from each other.

Members could be people from within your organization or leaders from outside. Meet regularly to discuss staff recognition. What are they doing? Is it working? What didn't work? What useful staff recognition resources have they discovered recently? Establish accountability by committing to what you will do to enhance staff recognition over the next few weeks. Report your progress the next time the group meets. See Conversation Starters for Book Clubs and Staff Recognition Mastermind Groups (p. 195) for suggestions of topics that mastermind groups could discuss.

***

If you are part of the leadership team in an organization with several managers (such as a school system, larger retailer, government office or health-care facility), suggest staff recognition as a topic for an all-managers meeting. What are other managers/leaders doing to recognize individuals and the whole team? Everyone will leave with new ways to recognize staff.

***

Add staff recognition to your next staff meeting agenda. Divide staff into groups to brainstorm ways they prefer to be recognized. Ask them to record their ideas on a flip-chart paper and post them around the room. By the end of the meeting, you will know more about how to recognize staff. **Bonus**: Staff will also gain insight into how to provide peer recognition.

***

Always be on the lookout for items that could be used to acknowledge staff for their contributions. Maybe it's a small souvenir you discover when travelling. Or it could be a unique gift or a "just-right" thank-you note. When you find an item that would be perfect for a particular staff member, buy it and set it aside until you have a reason to provide this special recognition.

***

Step away from your work environment to learn how others recognize staff. While attending a conference, visiting another workplace or during networking events, ask leaders from other organizations, "How do you recognize staff when they do their jobs well?" You may discover novel approaches to recognition that might work for you. Be prepared to share examples of what's working for you. Ideally, everyone will leave these conversations with at least one new way to say thank you.

***

What were your greatest staff recognition moments ever? It could be a time when you received recognition, or when the recognition you provided was particularly well-received. What did you learn from those experiences? How can you apply those lessons when you recognize staff in the future?

***

If gift cards are in your staff recognition tool kit, consider purchasing them from small businesses, such as independent bookstores, locally owned restaurants or neighbourhood coffee shops. These will help you express your appreciation and you will also be helping local business that may be struggling to survive.

***

> **A Final Thought**
> You don't need to have a lengthy list of staff recognition techniques. You just need a few. Master them to become effective. Occasionally, refresh how you recognize staff by finding other techniques to add to your staff recognition tool kit.

Theme #3
GREAT Staff Recognition: 5 Pieces that Make the Picture of Appreciation and Gratitude Complete

The acronym GREAT is a reminder that meaningful staff recognition consists of five ingredients: Genuine, Relevant, Explicit, Appropriate and Timely.

Recognition must be inspired by a **Genuine** sense of appreciation for how individuals or teams have contributed and what they have achieved.

After that, add one or more of the other ingredients to strengthen the impact of messages of appreciation and gratitude.

Recognition is **Relevant** when it's rooted in what the organization believes is important, often expressed in its mission statement, values and goals.

Recognition is **Explicit** when it includes specific descriptions of what the recipients did.

Recognition that is **Appropriate** respects the recipients' recognition preferences and reflects their interests.

Recognition will be **Timely** when it is delivered soon after the action that triggers recognition.

The more ingredients you include in a message of appreciation, the greater its impact.

These ingredients are discussed in more detail in the next few pages, with suggestions of ways to make staff recognition GREAT—**Genuine, Relevant, Explicit, Appropriate** and **Timely**. These ingredients are highlighted whenever they are referenced throughout the book.

Genuine: Ensuring Staff Recognition is Authentic

Why can some leaders recognize people in ways staff members value, while attempts by other managers to express gratitude fall flat? Why is it that when some leaders recognize staff it results in a boost to morale, increases engagement and improves retention, while what others do doesn't make a difference?

There is more to it than writing better thank-you notes, giving better gifts or choosing words of praise more wisely.

The value and effectiveness of staff recognition is not determined by what you do, but by *why* you do it, as judged by those being recognized. Recognition must be seen as inspired by a sincere sense of appreciation for what the recipients achieved or how they contributed.

In other words, recognition must be **Genuine**. It is the essential ingredient of meaningful staff recognition.

If recognition is not motivated by a sincere sense of appreciation—if it's not **Genuine**—the suggestions included in this and other books about recognizing staff will not work as you hope. Here are some ways to make it clear that your gratitude is **Genuine:**

Recognize people only when you sincerely believe they deserve to be recognized, not because "it's the thing to do" or because someone said you should recognize staff more (although you probably should).

***

Separate positive feedback from the negative, except when conducting performance appraisals, during which both are expected.

***

Ensure that your body language and tone of voice are in sync with your words of praise.

***

Be emotional. Show that the recognition comes from your heart. Let staff members know how good you feel about what they did.

Be consistent. Recognize what deserves to be recognized, no matter who did it, when or where. Never recognize what doesn't warrant recognition just because you feel bad that Joe has not been recognized recently. Wait and watch. His turn will come.

***

Keep it short and simple. The long, flowery presentations can seem artificial.

***

> **A Final Thought**
> Provide honest feedback. When someone screws up, tell them. When they succeed, tell them. This will make both types of feedback more believable.

Relevant: Making Staff Recognition Strategic

"Values are not just words, values are what we live by. They're about the causes that we champion and the people we fight for."

– John Kerry

Effective staff recognition begins with knowing what to recognize.

Staff members want to know what is expected of them. When staff understand what you expect—and when you want it done—they are more likely to do what you want them to do. Staff will be more engaged and work harder when they feel that what they do makes a difference.

The place to begin is with the documents that define the purpose of your organization. **Relevant** recognition links what staff members do to the organization's mission statement, values and goals.

> Seventy-seven per cent of employees surveyed by the Society for Human Resource Management in 2015 said that having a clear understanding of their organization's vision and mission was important to their job satisfaction and engagement.

Once created, mission statements, visions and goals are often lost in the general busy-ness of the workplace, never again to be read or discussed. Out of sight and out of mind, these documents that were meant to provide guidance become as irrelevant as a map tucked into a backpack that is not taken out and studied before a hiker ventures into the woods.

Recognition is a strategic tool that makes mission statements, values and goals **Relevant** to staff members every day. Use **Relevant** staff recognition to focus everyone on what's important:

Review your mission statement, values and goals. List behaviours that will move your organization closer to these outcomes. Share your list. Talk to staff about what's on the list. Praise people when you see them exhibiting these behaviours.

***

Involve others in defining what your organization's values look like in practice. Brainstorm with your leadership team to identify behaviours that reflect those values. What does "compassion," "innovation" or "risk-taking" look like? Ask staff to describe how they can reflect values such as "customer service excellence," "teamwork," "collaboration," etc., by what they do. Recognize staff for these behaviours when they occur.

***

When recognizing staff, explain how their contributions fit into the bigger picture. Remind them that what they do well is important because of how it reflects their organization's purpose. It helps the organization fulfil its mission and meet its goals and it satisfies the needs of customers. Emphasize that a teacher's action in the classroom contributed to student learning, or that a warehouse employee's effort resulted in orders being filled quickly, which created satisfied customers. What they do makes a difference!

***

Find reasons to recognize staff members by choosing just one value to focus on for a week. Observing behaviours reflecting that week's value should trigger recognition (but don't ignore other recognition-worthy actions when you witness them). When the week is over, assess what happened. Did you discover evidence of the value in action? How did you link recognition of what the staff member did to the value? Did you have opportunities to discuss the importance of the value? What value will you focus on next week?

***

Staff members may not always understand why they are being assigned specific tasks. Whenever possible, connect work assignments to the organization's mission statement, values and goals. Be clear about what each person is expected to do and how assigned tasks fit into the big picture.

***

Use recognition to show staff members that what they do makes a difference and is valued. People want to feel that they are doing meaningful work.

***

Reread your mission and values statements. Ask yourself: "Am I recognizing staff—or punishing them—for risk-taking, innovation, honesty, exceeding customer expectations, teamwork, continuous learning, etc.?" If "innovation" is one of your values, recognize those who find better ways to complete tasks associated with their work assignment.

***

Searching for reasons to recognize staff? Begin by asking yourself this question and answering it: "What do I want to see more of?" When you see staff members doing something on your list, you know it's time to recognize them.

***

Use more inclusive language ("we/us/our" versus "the company") when linking recognition to the organization's mission statement, values and goals. E.g. "The way you resolved that complaint demonstrated your commitment to *our* (not 'the company's') value of providing excellent customer service."

***

> **What's Being Recognized: Looking Busy or Being Productive?**
>
> Sometimes it's difficult to tell. Some people can look busy, without really achieving anything. Managers who fail to focus on the results that staff members achieve often praise people for busy-ness because it can be easier to see than outcomes. Recognition should acknowledge staff for doing what's important—efforts that reflect the values of the organization and help it achieve its goals.

During one-on-one meetings, highlight how each staff member's work contributes to the team or organization fulfilling its purpose, as expressed in the mission statement, values and goals. Ensure recognition is **Relevant** by linking the reasons for recognizing the staff member back to those foundation documents.

***

It's difficult for staff to understand what behaviours are **Relevant** if they do not know or understand the organization's purpose. Take time regularly to review its mission statement, values and goals and to discuss what they mean in a day-to-day context. Follow up by highlighting the connection between behaviours you are recognizing and the mission statement, value or goal when you recognize a staff member.

**

Create a "Core Values" award to be presented to staff members who act in ways that reflect the organization's purpose and values.

**

What should a job well done look like? You could answer this question yourself, or you could involve staff in defining what excellent work is. They know. Develop a consensus of which behaviours are **Relevant** to the team's success. Make a list and publish it. It will help staff better understand what is expected of them and the behaviours for which they will be recognized. Whenever you witness these behaviours, recognize the person or group that's responsible.

**

When you recognize staff in public and highlight the link between what people did and your organization's values and goals, you are reminding both the recipients and those who witness the recognition about your organization's purpose and what it believes is important. This helps focus everyone on what matters.

**

Create notepads with a checklist of the organization's values. Whenever you see behaviour that relates to one of the values, check it off and write a brief description of what you saw the person do, before handing the note to them.

**

When assigning tasks, encourage staff to ask questions. That ensures they have all they need to know to understand your expectations. The result will be a job well done and another reason to recognize staff.

**

> **A Final Thought**
> Phrase to praise: "What you did is important because . . ."

Explicit: Making Staff Recognition Specific

"Recognition is the highlighter pen of behaviour."

— Cindy Ventrice

Explicit may be the simplest of the ingredients of GREAT staff recognition to explain.

The Oxford Dictionary defines explicit as, "expressly stated or conveyed, leaving nothing merely implied; stated in detail." Other definitions include the phrase, "leaving nothing to the imagination."

> **Reasons to Recognize**
>
> What are some of the reasons you might recognize staff? Make a list of behaviours you want to encourage and keep it handy. Here are a few suggestions to get started:
> - Helping a colleague complete a challenging task
> - Completing a project on time and on budget (or early and under budget)
> - Creating a happy customer. Calming an upset customer
> - Suggesting a different approach to a routine task, which might be more efficient or more cost effective
> - Maintaining a positive attitude
> - Stepping up when someone is needed to complete a difficult or undesirable task
> - Providing leadership
>
> What can you add to your list?

Applied to staff recognition, this means being specific when describing what the recipient did. Simply saying, "You are doing a good job" without describing what the individual did falls short.

Explicit recognition shows that you are paying attention. It is evidence that you respect staff members as individuals. You care enough to learn about what they do and how their efforts contribute to your organization's success and the success of the staff member.

Explicit recognition reminds staff what is important and what they need to do to perform their jobs well. What gets acknowledged (because it is important and is done well) is what gets repeated. You will get more of what you praise.

Being **Explicit** allows you to recognize specific contributions by otherwise underperforming staff members. You are focusing on just one aspect of what they do, although other aspects of their work may not be up to par. Be clear that you are not providing an overall assessment. By recognizing praiseworthy behaviour when it occurs, you demonstrate fairness in your feedback. This small bit of praise could even help turn around their underperformance.

Use **Explicit** recognition to strengthen your messages of appreciation:

Set up staff members for success by communicating clear expectations.

***

Recognize outcomes (meeting pre-defined goals, completing a project on time, etc.) *and* conduct (listening to a patient's concerns, keeping filing up to date, etc.).

***

Create opportunities to celebrate success by encouraging staff members to set reasonable goals. Praise their efforts when the goals are realized. Success breeds more success.

***

Before giving in to the temptation to recognize staff with a general "Well done!" compliment, ask yourself, "Why am I thanking this person? What did they do that I feel warrants praise?" The answer will help you identify more reasons to provide **Explicit** recognition.

***

Use mnemonic devices to organize your message of appreciation:

> **SAR**—What was the **Situation**? What **Action** did the person take? What was the **Result**?
>
> **SAIL**—What was the **Situation**? What **Action** did the person take? What was the **Impact**? How did their action **Link** to the organization's values or goals?

A Final Thought

The amount of attention you pay staff has a powerful impact on their level of disengagement. The Gallup Organization found that when staff received positive input from leaders, disengagement was extremely low (only about one per cent). When feedback was negative, disengagement increased to 22 per cent. But when staff leaders were ignoring them, disengagement soared to 40 per cent.

Appropriate: Personalizing Staff Recognition

A key to meaningful recognition is knowing staff members as individuals.

This enables you to personalize staff recognition. You can express appreciation in ways that reflect staff members' interests, their preference for public or private recognition, and their need to be noticed and acknowledged.

Because the value of recognition is determined by the recipients, all three variables should be considered when deciding how, when and where to recognize staff. When you recognize staff in ways that reflect their interests and recognition preferences, you demonstrate they are valued, both as a person and as a staff member.

Much recognition, particularly formal recognition, occurs in public, in front of colleagues, friends and family. But many people prefer to be recognized in private. The value of recognition is diminished when the recipient feels uncomfortable being acknowledged in front of others. Some will go to great lengths to avoid public recognition.

> **Where to Recognize: Publicly or in Private?**
>
> To praise in public and criticize in private is good advice. Better advice may be to praise *both* in public and privately (but **never** criticize publicly). Even those who thirst after public recognition are unlikely to reject private praise. Also, in private is the best place to recognize shy introverts who may be uncomfortable receiving acknowledgement in front of their colleagues. It will also confuse those who believe that an invitation into the boss's office means the staff member is "in trouble." Turns out, this is no longer true if you start calling staff to your office to let them know how much you appreciate their outstanding contributions.

Avoiding all public recognition, such as the kind that occurs during staff meetings, may be difficult, but whenever possible find ways to respect people's wish to be recognized in private. You can do it in your office, during a visit to the recipient's work station, with a thank-you note left in the staff member's mailbox, or in an email.

Appropriate: Personalizing Staff Recognition

Some people need more recognition than others. Responding to this need is a challenge. Nevertheless, you need to satisfy those with a greater need for recognition, without recognizing others less frequently.

High-need people's thirst for recognition might be satisfied with simple gestures of appreciation delivered more frequently—a few simple words of appreciation written on a sticky note, in a text message or email, or a "pat on the back" when you meet in the hallway.

Use **Appropriate** staff recognition to personalize praise:

Learn what's important to staff members. Get to know each one's interests. Check out Theme #9: Discovering the Most Appropriate Ways to Recognize Staff (p 53) for ways to get to know staff members better.

***

Recognition that works in another work environment may not work in yours. Provide recognition that fits your organization's culture. Consider whether you can **Adopt** recognition practices you encounter, **Adapt** them for your circumstances, or if you should **Avoid** them See Tip #1: The 4 As of Staff Recognition (p xi).

***

When you know industrious employees devote much of their personal life to a not-for-profit organization in the community, reward them with a day off that they can spend by volunteering for that organization.

***

Surprise staff members with a special calendar or another small gift that reflects their interest in sailing, cats, cooking or other hobbies.

***

The right gift given to staff members to acknowledge their contributions is worth more than the cash value of the gift. A gift that shows you cared enough to discover how to personalize recognition means more to the recipient than an impersonal gesture of appreciation in the form of cash. A ten dollar gift card to their favourite coffee shop has more impact than a ten dollar bill.

***

A special coffee mug can help convey your appreciation. Show that you know recipients as individuals by filling the mug with their favourite treats or include a gift card for their favourite coffee shop. Strengthen this gesture of appreciation by beginning with a mug decorated with the recipient's favourite cartoon character or the logo of the sports team for which the recipient cheers.

***

Respect employees' recognition preferences. Some people hate being recognized in public. Don't announce awards publicly without first letting the recipients know of your plans. Offer the option to have the award presented to them out of the public view. If a public announcement is required, keep it low-key—in an email message to other staff or a brief newsletter article.

***

Try semi-private recognition. Rather than acknowledging publicity-shy staff members in front of the entire staff, deliver your message in the presence of just a few of the people with whom they work most closely and who know what they do every day.

***

Cancel generic gifts. Personalize the gifts you give staff, based on what you know about them—their non-work interests, career goals, favourite cartoon characters, etc. When staff members know that you know them as individuals it strengthens your message of appreciation.

***

Depending how they are used, gift cards can be an effective way to recognize staff, but many millions of dollars in gift cards go uncashed each year. Some may be misplaced or lost. Or it may be that the cards people receive are for businesses or products that don't correspond with their interests. Avoid the temptation to give every employee the same gift card, which makes the gesture less personal. Before giving another gift card, consider the intended recipient's interests and select an **Appropriate** gift card. Giving the right card shows recipients that you know them as individuals and you understand their interests.

- A coffee shop gift card for a caffeine addict
- A bookstore gift card for an avid reader
- A hardware store gift card for the person who always has a DIY project on the go
- Movie passes for the movie fan who sees every new release
- A gift card to an employee's favourite restaurant

***

A Final Thought
Recognition should fit your workplace culture. Consider age, profession, gender mix, religious and ethnic backgrounds and sexual orientation—all of which affect the personality of your team—when deciding how to recognize staff. For more on recognition in a diverse workplace, see Theme #22: Diverse and Inclusive: Recognition for Workplaces Where Everyone Feels They Belong (p. 126).

Timely: Putting Staff Recognition in the Moment

Does this seem familiar? You observe a staff member performing a task well and you think, "That's deserving of recognition. I'll do that . . . later."

You really intend to do it.

Later, you will have more time to acknowledge the person's contribution. Waiting allows time to figure out the best way to say, "Well done!" There will be time to write a thank-you note or to find a small token to express your appreciation.

But then life happens. You get even busier. A crisis demands your immediate response. Your praise goes unspoken and the contribution is forgotten.

Eventually, when there is a chance to say thank you, you begin, "I should have said something sooner."

Yes, you should have. Recognition too long delayed seems an insincere afterthought.

Worse yet, you say, "I can't remember what you did, but I know you did a good job of something."

When you don't remember what happened, providing **Explicit** recognition is impossible, whereas recalling the details would strengthen your message of appreciation.

Stop waiting for the perfect moment. Be spontaneous. Provide immediate feedback. When you see behaviour deserving of recognition, there's no reason to put off saying or doing something.

Let people know you saw what they did and appreciate their contribution while what happened is still fresh in both of your minds.

Smile. Give the staff member a pat on the back or a thumbs-up. Express your appreciation in a few words.

What you say or do may not be the most **Appropriate** way to recognize this individual, but immediate recognition sends a powerful message of appreciation.

Want to do more? You can always follow up on-the-spot recognition with another gesture, but when the recognition is **Timely**, something more may not be necessary.

Use **Timely** recognition to acknowledge contributions while memories are fresh:

Add "recognize staff" to your daily to-do list. Recognition should be part of every day.

***

Prepare to provide **Timely** recognition by stocking up on tools you will need to express appreciation when you witness actions that deserve to be recognized: thank-you cards, sticky notes, treats, small gifts, coffee shop gift cards, etc.

***

Schedule time to recognize staff—a time to write notes, send emails, make phone calls, or to drop by to say thank you. It could be a few minutes each day or an hour or two once a week. The longer you wait, the less meaningful the recognition becomes.

***

Emails or texts may be the most **Timely** way to recognize staff but don't always leave it at that. You can strengthen your message of appreciation by following up in person.

***

Being **Timely** doesn't mean recognition must always be instantaneous. Let a staff member know you would like to meet to provide positive feedback. "When would be a good time, tomorrow or the next day, for us to meet so that I can recognize you for what you did recently?" When staff members know praise is coming, the anticipation can increase the impact of your gesture.

***

Sometimes you can't recognize great work contributions in the moment. There are times when recognizing someone as soon as you see the praiseworthy behaviour may be inappropriate or awkward—you don't want to interrupt what the deserving employee is doing, you are on your way to an appointment for which you can't be late, or you are involved in a conversation with others (perhaps congratulating them on a job well done). Plan to connect with this staff member as soon as possible to recognize their contribution. Knowing that you made a special effort to return to say thank you can increase the impact of your message.

Here are some techniques to ensure that you follow through with your plans to recognize deserving staff members:
- Carry a small notebook in which to record what is needed to provide meaningful recognition: what the person did and why it is important
- Send yourself a reminder via email, text, or voicemail
- Put a reminder on your smartphone, or record a voice memo
- Jot the key information on a sticky note that you can stick to your desk, computer screen or wall where you will see it

***

A Final Thought
There is no statute of limitations on recognition—Most of us, at one time or another, have failed to give people recognition when we should have—which is soon after becoming aware that they had done a task well. We may have been distracted by other duties and now it seems too late to recognize the person. While ideally recognition should be **Timely**, being late is not a reason to forego praising someone. Even delayed recognition is better than no recognition at all. What's important is that it's motivated by a **Genuine** sense of appreciation.

Theme #4
Senior Executives, Frontline Staff and Recognition

If you are one of your organization's senior leaders, the next few pages are meant for you.

You certainly understand the importance of staff recognition. You have seen the research that shows staff value recognition from their senior leaders. You want to express appreciation to frontline staff but doing so is a challenge.

There may be several levels of management between you and those who are contributing on the sales floor, in classrooms, on hospital wards, or on construction sites.

Without firsthand knowledge about what individual staff members do, you may feel compelled to rely on formal staff recognition programs or general messages of appreciation, which frontline staff may not perceive as **Genuine**.

Given these circumstances, the more effective role for senior leaders may be to champion recognition throughout the organization. Try these ideas:

Start close to home. Become a staff recognition role model. Regularly recognize those who report directly to you. By acknowledging the contributions of your direct reports, you are modelling the behaviour you want to see from them. People who are recognized frequently are more likely to recognize others frequently.

***

Expect those who report to you to recognize those who report to them. Follow the example of one senior executive who let his managers know that he expected them to recognize staff. He created accountability by asking, "How have you recognized staff?" during one-on-one meetings.

***

Provide other leaders with what they need to recognize staff—training on how to recognize staff and resources to provide recognition.

***

Highlight your organization's culture of recognition when welcoming new members to the management/leadership team. Include staff recognition training as part of their orientation to prepare them for this aspect of their job. No leader within your organization should ever be able to use "I don't know how" as an excuse for not recognizing staff, nor for that matter, any of the excuses that are identified in Theme #27: How to Respond the Next Time Someone Says, "I Don't Recognize Staff Because . . . " (p. 150).

***

During leadership team meetings, discuss how to use staff recognition to boost morale, increase engagement and improve retention.

***

Celebrate those who do a good job of recognizing others.

***

Don't limit your contact with frontline staff to once-a-year staff recognition events, which may no longer be—and maybe never were—an effective way to let staff know they are valued as individuals and appreciated for what they do.

Visit workplaces regularly. Prepare by requesting information from managers and supervisors about how staff members contribute or what staff have achieved. Do the managers have messages they wish you to deliver to individuals or to the team during your visit? What contributions and achievements stand out?

***

When visiting the front line, show interest in what staff members are doing. Ask questions.

***

Invite customer feedback related to the contributions of individual staff members. Request that positive feedback be sent to you so you can add a few words of appreciation before it's forwarded to the staff member. See Theme #11: Mine Customer Feedback for More Reasons to Recognize Staff (p. 64), for suggestions on how to collect input from clients, customers and others.

***

If you still have staff recognition events, "work the crowd" during these gatherings. Engage in conversations with attendees. Don't just hang out with "your folks."

***

Encourage all members of your leadership team to read and discuss a book on staff recognition. Establish a staff recognition book club. What tools and techniques could your leaders adopt or adapt to recognize their staff? See Conversation Starters for Book Clubs and Staff Recognition Mastermind Groups (p. 195) for suggestions of topics for discussion during book club meetings.

***

Write messages of gratitude for frontline leaders to read during daily team huddles. As with all messages of appreciation, avoid being too general in your praise (it makes your message sound insincere). Be specific in describing what individuals or teams did that you appreciate.

***

Is retention important to your organization? Of course it is! So, what are you doing to recognize teams or departments with low voluntary turnover rates?

***

Contribute to building commitment of new staff members by being among the first to welcome them to the organization with a telephone call when they start or even before. Ask frontline leaders to provide the names and a contact number for new staff. Even a brief call from a senior leader will have a powerful impact.

***

Ensure all managers and supervisors have a budget for staff recognition.

Pass on to frontline leaders the staff recognition tips, tools and techniques you encounter.

＊＊＊

Ensure that the value of organization-wide staff recognition initiatives is assessed regularly. Are they working? What needs to be changed? Has the time come to retire an approach for acknowledging the contributions of staff members?

＊＊＊

> **A Final Thought**
> Effective staff recognition can begin anywhere in the organization, but when top leaders set the example, the commitment to staff recognition will spread more quickly.

Theme #5
Making Staff Recognition a Habit

Acknowledging the contributions and achievements of others must become more than a task to cross off your to-do list. Staff recognition needs to become a habit, which *Atomic Habits* author James Clear defines as "a behaviour that has been repeated enough times to become automatic."

The Canadian Oxford Dictionary takes its definition a step further, suggesting that habits are "acquired by learning and repetition." It takes commitment and practice to make recognizing staff an automatic behaviour—a habit. When recognition becomes a habit, you are well on your way to becoming the recognizer you hope to become.

Productivity expert Hugh Culver compares developing a habit to lighting a fire. "Just like a big fire, you have to start with a small flame. That's also how you create a new habit—start small."

There are loads of ways to start small before creating a staff recognition inferno:

Put "Recognize staff" at the top of your to-do list. Better yet, include the names of individuals whose contributions you wish to acknowledge. ("Recognize Liam for the way he managed the budget issue.")

***

Make it easier to recognize staff by building a staff recognition tool kit and keeping it close by. See Theme #2: "Filling Your Staff Recognition Tool Kit," (p.8) for suggestions of what to include.

***

Set time aside in your daily schedule to recognize staff. As little as fifteen minutes each day devoted exclusively to staff recognition will make an enormous difference to morale, engagement and retention.

***

Associate staff recognition with something you enjoy doing ("I will make myself a good cup of tea before sitting down to write thank-you notes") or reward yourself after recognizing staff. ("After writing three thank-you notes I will allow myself time to enjoy one chapter in the mystery novel I am reading.")[3]

***

Link staff recognition to an existing habit. ("I always follow up meetings with a summary of key decisions, after which I will write a brief note to anyone who contributed to the discussion.)

***

Improve the likelihood of achieving your goal to recognize staff more often by asking someone to become your accountability partner. Tell a friend, colleague, your boss or your administrative assistant about your intent to increase staff recognition and ask them to monitor your efforts to help keep you on track. Meet regularly to discuss what you have done to recognize staff.

***

Set daily targets and develop a simple way to keep score, such as tokens that you can move from one pocket to another every time you recognize someone. If your goal is to recognize three people per day, begin the day with three tokens in one pocket. Are all three tokens in the other pocket at the end of the day?

***

---

[3] This tip and the one that follows are based on two techniques from *Atomic Habits* by James Clear: the implementation intention formula and the habit stacking formula.

Leave yourself reminders to recognize staff—on a sticky note attached to your computer, as a voice mail that will be the first message you hear in the morning, or with a stack of thank-you cards on your desk.

***

Remove anything from your desk that may distract your attention from the task of recognizing staff.

***

Commit to writing one thank-you note daily.

***

List all your staff members on your weekly to-do list with the intent of crossing off each name during the week when you thank them for doing something you feel deserves recognition.

***

Spend at least two breaks each week with your staff or co-workers, with no agenda other than to listen and learn. Ask questions. Learn about them as individuals, how they do their jobs and what they do well.

***

Leaving your office at some point each day in search of reasons to recognize staff is a smart idea, but vary when you do this and the route you follow. Become too predictable and you will be inviting cynical staff to say, "Here comes Naomi. It must be time for her 3:15 recognition walk."

***

Put yourself in the mood to recognize staff by pausing to note what has gone well that day. Who was responsible for these successes? What did they do? Now that you know who did what, say thank you with a handwritten note, an email or words of appreciation the next time you see this person.

***

Even if you feel that you're not good at recognizing staff and that the recognition you provide seems to be missing the mark, don't give up. Keep trying. The more often you recognize staff, the better you will become at it. Recognizing staff will become a habit.

Before you leave at the end of the day, place a thank-you note and green pen (an upbeat colour for recognition notes) on your desk, where it will be the first thing you see the next day.

***

Set a modest goal to recognize each staff member at least once before the end of the month. Personalize the recognition by being specific about what they did and linking their performance to one of your organizational values. Later, you can increase your target to recognize each person at least once every two weeks or once a week.

***

> **A Final Thought**
> Opportunities to recognize staff are all around us if we look for them. Commit to finding opportunities to recognize staff members in every interaction you have with them. Begin small, by focusing on interactions that occur during the first hour of the day or during the half hour following lunch. Or spend one day each week finding reasons to recognize others. Soon, discovering reasons to recognize others will become a habit.

Section II
Using Your Staff Recognition Tools

There are hundreds of inexpensive and easy-to-implement ways to recognize staff, including thank-you cards, sticky notes and by linking staff recognition to career plans, family, the seasons, vacations, eco-friendliness, treats and more (including fun ways to recognize staff).

Theme #6
Staff Recognition's Number One Tool: Thank-You Notes

Thank-you notes increase the impact of your messages of appreciation, especially when they are handwritten. Not only is "the pen mightier than the sword," it also has a greater impact than the word processor or email. Handwritten words of appreciation always trump an email, text or other computer-generated message, even if the words used are exactly the same. A simple, handwritten note of appreciation appears more sincere than the most superbly crafted letter prepared on a computer screen.

It may take a bit longer to write a thank-you note than to just give someone a pat on the back, but the extra investment of time is worth it. Handwritten thank-you notes have staying power! They create an impression that lasts. Handwritten notes show that you value the recipients and what they did enough to personally invest your time to say thank you.

Recipients often hang on to handwritten thank-you notes. Some display them in their work area. They share them with their family and co-workers. They reread them, reminding themselves of their success and your gratitude for what they did. Here are ways to use staff recognition's number one tool:

Set a daily goal to write one thank-you note before the end of the day.

***

Keep a supply of thank-you notes where you will notice them frequently. Whenever you see them, ask yourself, "Who deserves to be thanked?"

Thanks, Again!

***

Convert waiting time into recognition time. Carry a supply of thank-you notes in your briefcase. Whenever you have a few minutes, such as when waiting for an appointment, when you're on an airplane, or when you are waiting for a meeting to begin, use the time to write notes to staff members who deserve to be recognized.

***

Double the impact of the positive, face-to-face feedback you provide by following up with a brief, handwritten note.

***

Any other colour of ink is better than black or red when writing thank-you notes. Why? Black makes your message look like one of hundreds that came from a photocopier. And we all remember what red meant when we were in school, don't we?

***

Take the concept of a handwritten note a step further—create a hand-drawn thank-you note. This highly personalized card could be your own artwork or something you commission your child or grandchild to design. Add your own words of acknowledgement and present a deserving employee with a unique card.

> **Do You Find Writing Thank-you Notes a Challenge? This template may help:**
>
> Dear _____.
>
> Thank you for __ (DESCRIBE WHAT THE RECIPIENT DID) __. __ (DESCRIBE HOW YOU FEEL ABOUT WHAT THE RECIPIENT DID) ___. What you did was important because it relates to __ (CITE A RELEVANT VALUE) ___, which is one of our core values. Your contribution/achievement is appreciated.
>
> Your signature

"I am a card-maker, so I will make a card to give to someone. The card is designed specifically for the person, the act, etc. It is handwritten and handmade."

– Seminar participant

Create company logo cards that are blank inside. Use them to write thank-you and other types of notes to both customers and staff.

***

Mail thank-you notes to the recipients' homes. In addition to staff members seeing your words of appreciation, their families will notice. Your hand-addressed envelope will stand out among all the bills and flyers. There will be questions when the staff member arrives home. "What's this about? Why did your boss send you a thank-you note?" It becomes an opportunity for recipients to share stories of their on-the-job success with family members.

***

While you could run the envelope through the postage meter at the office, you will increase the impact by using postage stamps. Your message will seem more personal, less "corporate." You could use regular-issue stamps, but your envelope will really stand out if you use stamps issued to celebrate special occasions, events, or achievements. Better yet, use stamps that relate to the recipient's interests, whether they are history, sports, nature or the lunar new year.

***

Turn a staff photo into a thank-you card.

***

Add an inspirational quotation to your thank-you note.

***

A Final Thought
Here's a final gift to slip beneath the Christmas tree for children on your list—a box of thank-you cards and a sheet of colourful stamps. On Boxing Day, encourage them to write notes expressing gratitude for what they received. Grandma, Uncle Don and other gift-givers will love receiving these cards and you will be contributing to developing future managers and supervisors who will understand the importance of saying thank you. This also works on birthdays or other celebrations at which gifts are received.

Theme #7
Recognition That Sticks

Sticky notes are a simple, quick-to-use and inexpensive staff recognition tool. Keep a supply on your desk or in your pocket so you can recognize staff spontaneously, anytime or anywhere. When you witness someone doing a task well, write a brief message of appreciation and stick it to anything—a desk, a tool kit or a computer screen. Here's how to provide recognition that sticks:

Sticky notes come in different shapes and colours. Reserve one shape or colour only for use when acknowledging and praising staff. Staff members will soon come to understand that a green circle or purple square attached to a desk or computer screen is an expression of your gratitude—even before they read your words.

***

Begin the week with a pad of sticky notes and a goal of leaving a brief expression of appreciation on every staff member's desk by Friday. Repeat regularly.

***

Attach messages of appreciation or congratulations to:
- Magazine or newspaper articles in which a staff member is profiled or quoted
- Positive letters or comment cards when customers identify specific staff members
- Well-written letters or reports prepared by staff members
- Individuals' favourite treats, encouraging them to take a well-deserved break

- Books by the staff members' favourite authors or on topics of interest to them

***

Make a newcomer feel part of the team with a welcoming note stuck to a box of business cards.

***

Invite existing staff to blanket the newcomer's desk with sticky notes welcoming the person on board.

***

Provide public recognition by sticking notes to a bulletin board where others will see them.

***

When they arrive for work, greet staff members with a note stuck to their desk or computer expressing gratitude for a contribution made the previous day.

***

Stick a note to a photograph of staff members at work before mailing it to their family: "Your parent/child makes important contributions to our business. We enjoy having him/her on our staff. Thank you for sharing him/her with us." Provide specific examples of how they have contributed.

***

Present a package of "super-sticky" notes to an employee, with a message that acknowledges the employee for "sticking with it" until they conquered a challenging task.

***

Create an instant coupon on a sticky note that an employee can exchange for a drink or treat in the company cafeteria. Describe what the staff member did that entitles the bearer to a complimentary beverage or treat.

***

Bundle evaluation forms collected at the end of a successful workshop that a staff member presented. But before you deliver them to the presenter, attach a sticky note on which you summarize the positive comments and add your own words of appreciation for a job well done.

***

> **A Final Thought**
> Remind yourself to recognize staff on a note attached to your calendar, computer screen or on your bathroom mirror.

Theme #8
Building Commitment from Day One

New staff can experience "buyer's remorse" within the first few days of starting a job: "Is this job right for me? Is this where I belong?" Newly hired staff members may begin thinking about searching for a new job much sooner than we think—as early as the first day on the job.

Much depends on their Day One experience. It's the source of first—and often lasting—impressions of a new employer, of new colleagues and, most importantly, of you, their new boss. It's within your power to influence whether fresh staff members begin to commit to your organization on Day One or start planning for a new job search.

The secret to building commitment from Day One is recognition. Let new staff members know they are valued and appreciated as soon as they are hired. Time you spend "re-recruiting" staff members during the first days and weeks on the job improves the likelihood that they will decide your workplace is where they belong and focus on what they were hired to do—and not on updating their resumes! Here are some techniques that you can use:

Begin early—even before Day One. Never delegate the task of making a job offer. The offer should come from someone that new hires perceive as significant within the organization, such as you, their soon-to-be supervisor.

***

While you should be the first, you need not be the only one they hear from. Encourage others to contact new hires. Imagine the impact when one of the first calls a new staff member receives comes from the CEO or another senior executive, just to welcome them to the organization.

***

You may be familiar with the adage, "Hire slowly. Fire quickly." This is good advice but can be improved by adding another phrase: "Recognize immediately." Find a reason to recognize new staff members on their first day. Did they master a new skill? Was there a positive encounter with a customer? How did they relate to co-workers? The reason may be small but the impact of your gesture will be huge. "The boss cares. The boss notices what I do. I feel valued for who I am and appreciated for what I do. This may turn out to be where I belong." No person should leave after the first day on the job having not heard any words of praise.

***

The first time you recognize a new staff member—ideally this should occur before the end of Day One—use this as an opportunity to ask about how the newcomer prefers to be recognized. In addition, take time to describe the organization's culture of recognition and to emphasize the role of all staff members in acknowledging co-workers for their support and for doing their jobs well.

***

Create a short questionnaire for new staff members to complete on their first day: what is their preferred name, recent employment or education background, family information (spouse's name, children's ages, etc.), non-work interests, etc. Ask their permission to share this information with the newcomer's colleagues. It could become the basis of conversations, or it could help create connections between the newcomers and existing staff based on common interests. What you learn about newcomers will also offer clues about **Appropriate** ways to recognize them.

***

Involve existing staff in planning the orientation of new staff. What do they need to know to succeed? What do you wish you had known on Day One? How should newcomers be welcomed to the organization? The insights of staff members who recently joined the organization may be particularly helpful.

***

Have everyone on the team sign a card to welcome a new person on their first day of work. Better yet, mail it to the new employee's home so that it arrives a few days prior to the first day. Enclose a photo of the team.

***

Greet new staff on their first day with a poster that welcomes them. Include a photo and a bit of the newcomer's background (where they worked previously, where they went to school, hobbies, etc.) to help existing staff get to know them.

***

Plan for the new staff member's arrival. Ensure that what they need will be available on Day One: business cards, a name badge, computer access and their name on internal directories. Nothing can feel worse on Day One than discovering that you weren't expected.

***

Let current staff know someone will be joining them. Provide background information about the newcomers—name, training and experience, start date and why you believe they will be an asset to the organization.

***

Show that you understand the importance of family. Welcome the staff member's family by sending a fruit basket or a bouquet of flowers to the new person's home. There's more to life than work.

***

You may know everyone who works with you and staff members know each other, but the new person won't know anyone's name. Even if it's not what they do regularly, encourage everyone to wear name badges for the first few days after someone joins the team.

***

Send new staff on a scavenger hunt, designed so that they will meet people with whom they will be working most closely and so they discover where to find the resources, tools and supplies they will need to do their job.

When introducing someone new, managers often refer to the employee bringing "new ways of doing things from which we can all learn and benefit." This can become an empty phrase if it's not followed by efforts to utilize what the newcomer knows. You can show you value the new staff member's opinion by requesting their input, ideas and suggestions and sharing what you hear with others. People are more likely to commit to a new employer when they feel their contributions are welcomed and recognized.

***

Adopt the practice of some retailers and coffee shops that give new staff members a badge that identifies them as new. This lets staff and customers know that this person has just joined the team and may not be sure how everything is done.

***

Welcome new staff members with a note attached to a treat or to a gift card to a nearby coffee shop. Highlight one skill that you discovered during the hiring process and describe how you feel the newcomer will be able to use that skill on the job.

***

Recognize existing staff members who help ease a newcomer's transition into your workplace.

***

Welcome new staff members with a handwritten note letting them know how pleased you are that they joined your organization.

***

Invite a current staff member to serve as a mentor for the new staff member. They can respond to questions that come up. They can clue newcomers into those important little details that never seem to be part of the official orientation. After a few weeks, meet with both the mentor and newcomer to see how things are going.

***

Stay Interviews

At regular intervals during their first year, schedule stay interviews with new staff members. Stay interviews are a proactive approach to improving staff retention. Use these one-on-one conversations to learn what they like about their work and what could be done to keep them on the team. You could ask:
- What do you like about your job?
- Is the job meeting your expectations?
- What do you wish you had known before taking this job?
- What has surprised you about this job/our organization?
- What factors contribute to your enjoyment of this job or cause you to stay in the job?
- If someone asked you about working here, what would you say?
- Do you feel that what you do makes a difference?
- Do you feel "fully utilized" in your current role? If not, what would make you feel fully utilized? What can we do to take advantage of your talents and interests more fully?
- What things do you really miss from your last job? What did you like doing in your previous job that you are not doing here?
- What are the less desirable elements or sources of frustrations in your current role? What do you wish you could do less of?
- In what ways have you been recognized that made you feel more motivated in your job?
- What challenges have you faced in this job? How did these make you feel about the job?
- What caused you to leave your last two jobs? Are there factors from your previous jobs that you hope you will never have to experience with this organization?
- What don't you like about your job?
- What do you most look forward to when you come to work?

Consider scheduling stay interviews for all staff every year or two. What you learn may help you identify ways to improve a work environment as well as staff retention. You will need to vary the questions you ask longer-term staff.

Arrange for a mentor/buddy to greet newcomers with a welcome gift, such as a mug bearing the corporate logo, a vest, cap or T-shirt.

***

Arrange for everyone to gather for coffee and muffins on a new staff member's first day. Ask a few staff members to take the newcomer to lunch.

***

Do you know some positives about the new staff member? You sure do, based on what you learned during the interview that led to your decision to make a job offer. Let them know why they were hired. What information from their resume impressed you? What did you hear during the interview that convinced you that they were the one? How will the organization benefit from having them on staff?

***

During the first week, arrange for the new employee to drop by other staff members' workspaces to deliver doughnuts or other treats. This activity will create another reason for the new person to interact with colleagues.

***

When a new employee joins the organization, calculate when the newcomer will reach certain milestones—30 days, two or three months, 100 days. Plan to mark these occasions by highlighting what the person has learned and achieved since Day One. Involve others in the celebrations.

***

When it comes time to celebrate new staff members reaching certain employment milestones, highlight how their actions during their first month or 90 days are **Relevant** to one of the organization's core values.

***

Spread out the orientation. Be selective about what and how much information you give new staff members. It's not necessary to tell new staff everything they will ever need to know on Day One. There is a limit to how much anyone can absorb at one time. Provide enough information about specific aspects of the job to enable new employees to begin to contribute.

Schedule additional training and orientation sessions over the next few weeks and months.

***

Make a discussion of the organization's culture a part of the on-boarding process. Emphasize the beliefs and values that guide people's actions. You are laying the groundwork for **Relevant** staff recognition.

***

Allow newcomers to contribute immediately. Your new employees believe they were hired due to their skills and knowledge. They are eager to get started, to demonstrate what they can do. Too much time spent completing forms, studying procedure manuals and memorizing policies and guidelines will soon diminish the enthusiasm of even the most energetic newcomers. Create opportunities for them to contribute somehow, even if it is in a small way.

***

The first time you recognize staff members, do so in private because you don't know how new staff members will respond to recognition. They may be okay with public recognition, but not everyone is. Being recognized in public, especially in front of people they have just met, may make them uncomfortable. Creating an experience that the recipient finds excruciating will overpower the feeling of feeling appreciated that you hoped to create.

***

When introducing existing staff members to newcomers, include a brief description of their skills and talents and how they contribute to the organization. The newcomer will learn who to go to for information or advice, and you will have provided a bit of recognition to existing staff.

***

As important as it is that you, the supervisor, are there to greet the new staff member at the beginning of the day, it is equally important that you spend time with them near the end of the day. Discuss the day. Ask questions: "How was your day? What did you learn today? How were you able to contribute? What questions do you have about our organization?" This is also a good time to provide specific, positive feedback on something you saw the newcomer do well.

***

Ask new staff members how they want to be addressed and, in some cases, how to pronounce their name. Do they prefer Jim or James, Catherine or Cathy, Bill or William? This is the name to use when introducing them to co-workers and customers. People's names are music to their ears.

***

> **A Final Thought**
> Recognizing a new person on Day One is just the beginning. If you keep the recognition coming, you will be taking an important step toward improving staff retention. No one wants to have a new staff member decide to become a short-term employee.

Theme #9
Discovering the Most Appropriate Ways to Recognize Staff

We all know the golden rule: "Do unto others as you would have done unto you." More important in the context of staff recognition is the *platinum* rule: "Do unto others as they would have done unto them." The recognition staff members value may be different than the recognition you value.

No two people are exactly alike. Finding **Appropriate** ways to recognize them acknowledges their uniqueness.

Get to know the people with whom you work. When you understand what's important to staff members and what's happening in their lives, it is easier to find **Appropriate** ways to recognize them. How do they spend non-work time (hobbies, travel, volunteering)? Which do they prefer, coffee or tea? Red wine or white? What are their career goals? Where do they prefer to be recognized, in public or in private?

Use what you discover about staff members to decide how to recognize them—to do unto them *what they would have done unto them:*

Learn from Staff Members' Previous Recognition Experiences: During one-on-one conversations ask staff members, particularly those new to the team, to: "Describe your most memorable recognition experience. What makes it stand out?"

If necessary, ask follow-up questions:
- Is this the type of recognition you prefer to receive?

- What might have been a better way for your boss/colleague to have recognized you?
- Where do you prefer to be recognized? Publicly or in private?

The answers will yield insight into **Appropriate** ways to recognize them.

***

Note what staff members display on their desks or post in their workstations. Ask about photos, certificates or souvenirs. You are showing your interest in them as individuals, not just as employees. What they display and what they say about these items may be clues to **Appropriate** ways to recognize them.

***

Listen to staff members' expectations and aspirations. What do they tell you about how to recognize them?

***

> **Do You Know Your Staff?**
>
> What if your boss stops by and asks you to introduce each staff member? Could you provide this information about each staff member?
> - Name
> - How long they have been with the company
> - Role on the team
> - Special strengths they bring to the team
> - Current project and why it is important
>
> If you don't have all this information top of mind, work on it. Great leaders really know the people on their teams. Knowing who they are and what they do well creates the basis for recognition.

Not sure how staff members prefer to be recognized? Ask them. Bring it up during one-on-one meetings. Ask them on their first day. You could even ask about recognition during hiring interviews. Have them list how they prefer to be acknowledged for doing their jobs well. Add a question to a staff survey. Make it a topic for discussion at your next staff meeting. Use whatever you learn to personalize the recognition that you provide.

***

Ask a staff member or someone from outside your organization to lead a brainstorming session with their colleagues to answer the question: "What are the best ways to recognize staff for how they contribute and what they achieve?" Have this facilitator leave a list on your desk to guide you when recognizing staff.

***

Commit to having a conversation with each employee during the next two weeks. Your goal for these conversations will be to learn something new about each person—hobbies, children's names, volunteer activities, leisure time activities, etc. How can you use this information to recognize this staff member?

***

Reflect on how you have recognized staff in the past. How have they received the recognition? What seemed meaningful to them, and what didn't? What have they done with awards and certificates, thank-you notes, or small gifts? Your observations may lead you to abandon some practices and replace them with more **Appropriate** ways to recognize staff.

***

To what type of recognition do recipients respond most favourably? Provide more of this type of recognition.

***

Ask new staff members to recall a time when they were recognized in a way that made them feel particularly appreciated. The answers will help you decide how to recognize them in the future. (You could do this with existing staff, as well).

***

Randomly select staff members to join you for coffee or lunch. Use the time to learn more about them as individuals and about what they do at work. You will discover reasons to recognize them and **Appropriate** ways to deliver this recognition. Repeat with other staff.

***

What do you know about individual staff members? Focus on one person at a time. Do you know enough to be able to personalize the recognition you provide?

***

To learn how to best recognize staff, ask individual staff members, "What do you feel would be the best way to recognize your colleagues?" Chances are that the answer will include hints about how to best recognize the person from whom you are seeking advice.

***

Check staff members' social media profiles to learn more about their interests—information that can serve as a guide to **Appropriate** ways to recognize them.

***

During a meeting, ask staff members to share one thing about themselves: a great book they read, a favourite snack, or where they volunteer. Use what you learn to identify **Appropriate** ways to recognize them.

***

Try this little staff recognition experiment. Before offering the choice from two tokens of appreciation, predict to yourself which one the recipients will select. Was your prediction accurate? The greater the accuracy of your predictions, the better you know the individuals and the more **Appropriate** the recognition you provide is likely to be.

***

7 Questions to Ask to Recognize Staff Appropriately

Use these questions to get to know individual staff members better. Ask them during individual conversations in your office, over coffee in the break room, or at employees' workstations. Each question is followed by suggestions about how to use what you learn to recognize staff appropriately:

1. **How do you like to spend your non-work time?** When you know about employees' hobbies and other interests, you can use this information to reinforce your words of appreciation with a small item related to a hobby or interest—a sailing calendar for a sailboat enthusiast, a cookbook for someone who loves to prepare gourmet meals, or a sleeve of balls for a golfer. Your gesture will demonstrate that you know and value them as individuals, as well as for their contributions to the organization.

2. **What are your career goals? (Or what would you like to learn more about?)** When you stop by to congratulate staff members on a job well done, stay a little longer to talk about where they see themselves in a few years' time. Provide work assignments or learning opportunities that will help them develop skills or gain knowledge that will prepare them to make their next career move.

3. **What charities do you support?** Cash is not a particularly effective tool with which to recognize staff. Even if it was, most organizations could not afford to pay bonuses that were large enough to be meaningful. But a few dollars donated to a charity of the employee's choice—*not* one selected by the manager—will be appreciated by both the staff member and the charity that receives the donation. By linking recognition to what people care about, you value the recipient as a person as well as someone who does a good job.

4. **Who is your favourite cartoon character/actor/athlete/recording artist?** Whenever an employee sips coffee from a mug bearing Minnie Mouse or Superman's image, it will be a reminder of your gratitude for a task completed ahead of schedule. Seeing their favourite actor's latest movie will be more special when your words of thanks are accompanied by a movie pass. Listening to a CD

by a favourite artist will remind the employee how sweet your praise sounded.

5. **What do you like to read?** Ask if they have a favourite magazine, author or genre. Say thank you with a subscription to a magazine that the employee will enjoy reading. Purchase an author's latest novel and leave it on the employee's desk with a note expressing gratitude for a contribution to the organization's success.

6. **How do you like to be recognized? In public—or in private?** The answers to these and similar questions will reveal the employee's recognition preferences. How you recognize individual staff members should reflect your understanding of these preferences.

7. **What is your favourite treat?** When someone has been working particularly hard, surprise them with their favourite treat. Deliver it in person or leave it on their desk. Add a note expressing appreciation for their hard work or willingness to put in the extra time required to complete a project on schedule.

> **A Final Thought**
> Should recognition be delivered publicly or in private? There's no right answer, because it depends. What are the recipients' recognition preferences? Some people are energized by being recognized before a large audience, while others are terrorized by the prospect. While it's important to discover each employee's preference, not knowing is no reason not to acknowledge contributions. You will never go wrong with recognition that's delivered in private. Even those who like others to witness their recognition still appreciate knowing that you know what they do and value their contributions.

Theme #10
Linking Staff Recognition to Career Goals

"Train people well enough so they can leave, treat them well enough so they don't want to."

– Richard Branson

One of the commonly asked questions during interviews should be left until after a person is hired: "What are your career goals?" Asking this question of newly hired people and existing staff could lead to discovering **Appropriate** ways to recognize them.

Linking recognition to career goals makes a position more than "just a job." It becomes a gateway to the future for your staff. Giving them opportunities for career advancement by helping them acquire the knowledge and skills necessary to move forward may actually improve your ability to retain top performers. Demonstrate you care about them and their futures:

Meet one-on-one with newly hired—and current—staff members to learn about their plans. What are their career aspirations? Where do they hope to be in five or ten years? Explain that you are committed to helping staff grow their careers. Use what you learn from these conversations when you recognize them.

***

Always be prepared to help those who work hard to achieve their career goals. Provide them with opportunities to take on tasks which will require them to develop new skills or will raise their profile within the organization.

Encourage them to apply for promotions when they become available, even if that means you may lose a top performer.

***

Show your interest in staff members as individuals by talking with them about their career expectations. Is there some way you can assist them to meet those expectations? If their expectations can't be met within your organization, your honesty is important. Explain why it's not possible.

***

Offer mentoring—by yourself and others—to assist staff members to fulfil their dreams.

***

Acknowledge staff members for what they do that moves them closer to their goals.

***

Reward their contributions with opportunities to learn new skills that will enable them to achieve the future they envision.

***

Express appreciation by inviting staff members who consistently do their job well to step outside their comfort zone. Is there something new they would like to try their hand at, temporarily? This will be a chance for them to master new skills that will make them a greater asset to your organization and will further their career development.

***

Before assigning a task, reflect on how it might relate to an individual's career goals. Explain how you considered their goals before selecting them to take on the task.

***

Recognize people by giving them authority. Invite them to run a meeting, to head up a project, to control a budget, or to decide which piece of equipment to buy. Think about how the assignment links to their career goals.

***

When marking service anniversaries, focus less on the fact that the employees have hung around for five years and more on how their career has developed over time.

***

Invite staff members to share with their colleagues one career-related goal they are working toward. Encourage their colleagues to look for opportunities to cheer their co-workers on or to celebrate the goal's successful achievement.

***

Connect staff members who have similar career goals and interests. This demonstrates that you understand their goals and you want to create opportunity for them to learn from each other.

***

Provide opportunities for staff to talk with senior leaders about their career goals.

***

Use one-on-one meetings to discuss staff members' progress toward their career goals. If they raise concerns about not having received promotions, provide feedback and suggest what they can do to better prepare.

***

For each of their career goals, ask staff members to prepare two lists. A: What the staff member already knows and, B: What they

> **Invest in the Professional Development of Top Performers**
>
> Managers and supervisors spend too much money and time in futile efforts to improve the skills of underperformers who seldom seem to benefit from these learning opportunities. Often, there seem to be fewer of these opportunities for top performers. Change this in your organization by expressing appreciation for tasks that are consistently done well, with opportunities to attend seminars and conferences that are related to the learning desires and career aspirations of top performers. They will appreciate the chance to enhance their skills, and your organization will benefit when they apply what they learn to their jobs. The Gallup Organization found that one of the 12 predictors of successful organizations (those that are productive and profitable with high customer satisfaction and low staff turnover) is that employees respond in the affirmative when asked, "Is there someone at work who encourages your development?"

still need to learn to achieve their goals. What can they do to shift items from column B to column A? How can you help this happen?

***

Meet with a staff member whose performance you feel is unsatisfactory. Suggest creating a professional growth plan. Begin with the staff member's career goals. What does the person need to do to reach these goals? How can you assist? What resources can you provide or suggest? Help the staff member find a mentor. Arrange for the staff member to attend a training program. Provide time off for study. Plan to meet with the staff member regularly to review progress, celebrate successes and adjust the plan as required.

***

Provide "scholarships" to acknowledge contributions, which the recipient can use to pay for a work-related course, to attend a conference, or for a general interest continuing education program.

***

Whose brain would they like to pick? Express appreciation by arranging an opportunity for staff members to have a one-on-one meeting with someone within the organization they would like to meet—this gives them time to ask questions, to receive advice or to be mentored.

***

Provide opportunities for staff to learn from each other. Did someone develop a unique solution to a problem, a new way to complete a routine task, an idea to save time or money, or a better approach to serving customers? Invite them to present their idea to the rest of the team.

***

When staff members show an interest or ability related to a specific task, provide more opportunities for them to practise this skill.

***

Thinking of creating a professional development library for your staff? Great idea. You likely have several titles in mind that your staff would benefit from reading. But don't limit the library just to your reading choices. Invest in staff members' professional development by purchasing books for the organization's resource library that staff feel would help advance their career development.

***

Both managers and the people they supervise are frequently apprehensive about annual performance reviews and approach them with reluctance. As a manager, you can change that. Show enthusiasm for the process. Let staff know that your intent is to find examples of what they do well and identify opportunities for growth—for which you will provide support. Demonstrate your commitment to providing timely feedback by setting a realistic appraisal schedule and sticking to it.

***

Do you have an expert, such as a consultant or speaker, visiting your organization? Express your gratitude for a task well done by scheduling time for a staff member to meet with the visitor.

***

> **A Final Thought**
> Encouraging and supporting staff as they pursue professional goals is important because it helps them become more effective on the job. But don't limit what you do to professional goals. When you encourage and support them in pursuit of personal goals, it shows that you care about them as people.

Theme #11
Mine Customer Feedback for Reasons to Recognize Staff

> *"We always try to share guest feedback with our teams because it is very important for them to hear how what they do each day actually does impact our guests, both positively and negatively —although, I must admit, I do enjoy sharing the positive feedback more."*
>
> – Kenneth Ells, guest services supervisor, Marriott Hotel, Halifax, Nova Scotia

A few years ago, throughout the Lambert-St. Louis airport, posters invited travellers to "Nominate an Airport Employee Today" for providing "Great Customer Service." This is one example of how organizations collect feedback from clients, customers and others.

Frontline leaders can learn from customers and others what staff members are doing for which they should be recognized. There are many ways to collect and use the words of others to acknowledge staff for what they do:

When you receive positive feedback from a customer, pass it along with your congratulations for a job well done.

***

Follow the example of a school district that asked survey respondents to, *"Think about a staff member who has meant the most to you during your school career. What made this person special to you?"* Hundreds of individual comments were collected, sorted and shared with the teachers and support staff identified by the students and parents.

***

Costco subtly encourages positive feedback by posting notes received from customers where both staff and other customers will see them.

***

Whenever positive comments are posted at online business-rating sites, bring these to the attention of staff.

***

When a positive story appears in the local media about one (or more) staff members or about your organization itself, ensure that everyone involved receives a copy of the newspaper or magazine article. Share links to radio or television stories. Let staff know how pleased you were to see the report.

***

Remind staff of the satisfied customers they have served that day by asking at the end of their shift, "What feedback did you receive from customers today? With what aspects of their experience were they most satisfied?" You may hear about complaints but you will also hear the positives, which you can reinforce.

> "A principal showed up at my door while I was teaching because he overheard a couple of students talking excitedly about the class that was about to occur. He stayed to observe the class for a while, thanking me in front of the students before he left."
>
> – A comment from a teacher, submitted anonymously

***

Add this question to customer satisfaction surveys: "Is there a person whose commitment to customer service stands out in your mind? What did they do that made your encounter memorable?" Share the positive comments you receive with the individuals who customers identified. Add a few of your own words of praise.

Extend the practice of providing customers with comment cards one step further, by inviting them to identify staff members who have served them well. You can even suggest aspects of the service you provide which staff members may have done well, as the Lambert-St. Louis airport did by inviting comment in the following categories: Making Your Day, Joyful Attitude, Solving a Problem, Great Service, Pride in Performance, Respectful Attention, Exceptional Effort and Going Above and Beyond. Echo what the public says by adding a few comments of your own before sharing the customer feedback with staff members.

***

Find reasons to recognize staff by asking customers or clients to "describe a time when you received outstanding service from someone on our team." Share what you hear with the person responsible for this great service.

***

When you receive positive feedback from customers, ask them to put it writing so that you can share it with staff. They may agree to do as you suggest, although many will not follow through. A better approach might be to do it yourself. Write down what you heard and pass it along to the person or team responsible for pleasing the customer.

***

Display letters of appreciation from customers somewhere where staff will see them. Reinforce the customers' messages with your own handwritten words of appreciation or praise.

***

If you are copied on an email in which a colleague or someone on your staff is recognized, add your own words of praise or congratulations or even just a smiling face or thumbs up emoji and forward the email to the original recipient.

***

Has your organization or department received high satisfaction scores on a customer survey? Let staff know and thank them for contributing to these results. It's worth celebrating.

***

When you receive a positive note from a customer—particularly if the customer identifies the staff member with whom they are pleased—share the message with the staff member. Ask permission to share with others. Post it on a bulletin board. Read it out at a staff meeting. Publish it in an internal or external newsletter. The customer didn't name the staff member? That's OK. You can still post, read or publish the message. The staff member (and others) will figure out who the customer had in mind.

***

When you receive positive input from a customer, consider inviting the customer to visit the workplace or to attend a staff meeting to deliver the praise in person.

***

During "morning huddles," read positive comments from happy customers. It gets the day off to a great start!

***

A Final Thought
Listen carefully when customers praise staff members' actions. They are telling you what is important to them and why they continue to do business with you. Are these the same behaviours for which you recognize staff?

Theme #12
Vacation-Themed Staff Recognition

Everyone is entitled to vacation time. It may be required by legislation or provisions of collective agreements, but for most staff members vacation time is more than that—it's deserved. Staff members have earned their paid time off, not because they have put in the requisite time but because of how they have contributed and what they have achieved since their last vacation. Let them know how you feel before they leave:

In private conversations before staff members begin their vacation, let them know that you feel they *deserve* time away from work. Highlight recent contributions and achievements that you particularly appreciate.

***

Send staff members off with intriguing reading material—a guidebook for a country that they will be visiting or something new from their favourite author or genre. But don't hand them a book on a work-related topic. They're supposed to be relaxing on the beach, not thinking about the job.

***

Encourage staff to bring back postcards to add to a display of vacation destinations. Suggest that they also post vacation photos. These will generate conversations for months to come.

***

If you know where staff members will be staying while on vacation, mail a brief note, care of the hotel, with a request that it be held until your staff member checks in. What a surprise to have your message waiting when they arrive. "Hope you have a restful vacation. You work hard and deserve a break. Enjoy yourself."

***

Prepare for Post-Vacation Recognition: Suppose that soon after Gavin left for a two-week vacation, you discover that he made an important contribution just prior to his leaving. Prepare to recognize him when he returns by adding a reminder to your calendar to speak to him. To avoid having difficulty remembering the details of what Gavin did, jot down a description of it now. Lots will happen while he is away.

***

Welcome Back Message #1: When staff members return from vacation, welcome them back and let them know they were missed and why: "You are someone to whom other staff know they can go to for answers about procedures, products or customers. You offer creative solutions to problems we encounter. You have a positive influence on our team. You have an ability to put things in perspective."

***

Welcome Back Message #2: "Here's why you *weren't missed*: Before you left, you tied up as many loose ends as possible so there were no surprises for those who remained behind. When it wasn't possible to wrap up a project before you left, you prepared your colleagues for what might come up during your absence so that they were forewarned."

***

Schedule time for staff members to answer the big questions: "How was your vacation? Where did you go? What did you do?" It's an opportunity to share photos, to show off souvenirs and to talk about their experiences.

***

When staff return to work do more than ask, "How was your vacation?" Hold a fun contest and give awards to the staff member who travelled the furthest (both in a straight line from home and the total number of kilometres travelled), had the most unexpected vacation experience, provides the best reason for a staycation, offers the best reason to return to a destination visited previously and, for those who didn't take a summer vacation, has the best reason to delay their vacation until later in the year.

***

Rather than asking, "How was your vacation? Where did you go? What did you do?" change the focus to the future. Ask, "Where do you hope to go next?" People look forward to their next vacation. Planning for an upcoming trip can energize them. Provide **Appropriate** recognition by feeding on their passion with a gift that relates to their future vacation: a travel guide, a link to an informative website, etc.

***

While you are on vacation replace the "wish-you-were-here" cliché with a "glad-you're-not-here" postcard to those back at the office: "Knowing that you are looking after things back at work makes it easy for me to relax and enjoy my time off."

***

Which staff members would you prefer were never on vacation at the same time as you are? Who are you confident will keep things moving smoothly in your absence? Who makes you feel you are leaving the organization in good hands? Do they know how you feel? Make sure they do. Tell them!

***

> **A Final Thought**
> Praise staff members who pick up the slack when a co-worker is on vacation. They are the ones who keep everything on track while others are away.

Theme #13
Include Family Members in Your Staff Recognition Plans

Your staff recognition practices can reflect your understanding that family is important to staff members. This will make a difference to both staff members and to your organization.

The more that staff members' families understand about what employees do, the importance of their contributions, and how they are appreciated for what they do, the more supportive they will be—especially at times when their family member must work extra hours, bring work home or travel on business. When people have family support, it is easier for them to focus on their work.

Write a letter of appreciation to staff members' families, explaining the importance of the work they do. Note a time when the staff member put in extra effort, worked late to complete a significant project, or travelled on company business. Express thanks for the support they provide to their parent, partner or child.

***

Make Parents Your Staff-Retention Allies: Send a note to the parents whose children are your staff members. Let them know how richly you appreciate the ways their offspring contributes. Be specific. Congratulate them for the fine job they did in raising the person with whom you are proud to work. It won't take long for your praise to get back to your staff member. As a bonus, you may even be creating staff-retention allies. The next time a son or daughter says it's time to look for another job, a parent who recalls your words might ask, "Why would you leave a place where you are appreciated? It seems to be where you belong."

***

Any time you meet members of a staff member's family, use it as an opportunity to praise the contributions of the staff member. "Did your son tell you how he solved a customer's problem last week? He asked great questions to learn more before he proposed a solution. The customer was satisfied with the solution your son suggested and went away happy. I am convinced that that customer will be back soon thanks to your son." The parent will feel pride and your words will soon reach the ears of your staff member.

***

In an ideal world, all mothers would be able to spend the Mother's Day with their children, but many mothers will be required to work that day (and fathers on Father's Day). Show appreciation to those mothers who must leave their families to come to work, with a corsage to wear on Mother's Day (and a boutonniere for fathers on Father's Day).

***

Provide an opportunity for staff members to spend a little extra time with their families by sending them home early on the Friday prior to the Family Day weekend (observed in several Canadian provinces). No Family Day where you live? No problem. This gesture of appreciation will work prior to any long weekend when staff would appreciate the opportunity to spend more time with their families.

***

Say thank you with the gift of an activity that will involve family members (dinner at their favourite restaurant, movie passes, tickets to a sporting event or concert, a board game everyone can play, a jigsaw puzzle, etc.) if work has required a staff member to spend an extraordinary amount of time away from home (overtime, business trips, etc.).

***

Say thank you to staff members who are parents with the gift of time—to attend a school concert, to volunteer in a child's classroom, or to just hang out with the kids on a day when they don't have school.

***

Invite family members to attend ceremonies where staff members will receive awards to celebrate what they have achieved or how they contribute.

***

Ask staff members for the names and birthdays of their immediate family. Show you understand the importance of family with a card (or a small gift) to family members on their special day. Include a message explaining why you appreciate having their partner, parent or child on your staff.

***

Include families in celebrations of team successes. Invite them to attend ceremonies where staff members will receive awards. Schedule a picnic or barbeque which the entire family can attend.

***

Send flowers or another small gift to staff members' partners when they have had to work extra hours on a big project.

***

Invite family members to a family day at your workplace. This will provide an opportunity for them to see where their parent, partner, or child works and learn more about what they do.
- Send invitations to the event directly to family members. Let staff members know what is happening, but don't make them your messengers. The invitations will seem more significant when they come from you.
- Greet family members as your guests when they arrive
- Display photos of family members on the job
- Tell your guests how their family members contribute and highlight why these contributions are important to the success of your business

***

Show your interest in staff members' families by attending their children's concerts or by dropping by their hockey or soccer games.

***

Pay for babysitters so staff members and their significant other can go out for a date night.

***

Acknowledge the importance of family support to staff members' success with recognition that the recipient can take home, such as a flower bouquet to share with the family, a family movie pass or a gift card to a family restaurant.

***

> **A Final Thought**
> Key dates to incorporate into your family-related staff recognition plans:
> - Family Day (observed on the third Monday of February in Alberta, British Columbia, Ontario and Saskatchewan)
> - Mother's Day—second Sunday of May
> - Father's Day—third Sunday of June
> - Grandparents' Day—second Sunday of September

Theme #14
Important? Certainly. But Recognition Can Be Fun, Too

"People rarely succeed unless they have fun in what they are doing."

– Dale Carnegie

Recognition is important and should be taken seriously, but that doesn't mean it can't also be fun. Staff members will enjoy silly and playful awards—many of which depend on puns that make you laugh or groan. Fun recognition that generates smiles and laughter has a positive impact on the workplace. It helps build relationships and boost morale. Having fun at work increases engagement.

Besides being tangible symbols of your gratitude, fun awards make messages of appreciation memorable and can have more lasting value than staid, serious awards:

Rather than relying on the generic title "receptionist," one company designated the person who greets visitors and answers the phone as the "Manager of First Impressions," which accurately describes how she contributes. Who in your organization deserve job titles that better capture the value of their contributions? Why not invite staff to come up with titles that capture the essence of their work?

***

Remember recess? Best part of the school day, wasn't it? Everyone looked forward to getting outside to play with friends in the sunshine. Say thank you to your hardworking team by sending them outside for a break. Once there, who knows what might happen? A game of Frisbee might break out. Other people may simply enjoy the fresh air and blue sky for a rejuvenating interlude before heading back to their desks.

***

Pop Goes the Recognition! Slip a few words of praise into a balloon before inflating it. When staff members pop the balloon, they will discover your words of appreciation.

***

The comic strips in your daily newspaper can be a source of staff recognition inspiration. Look for cartoons to help convey your messages of appreciation. Something a character did or said may remind you of what a staff member did or might relate to one of their non-work interests. Write a message on a sticky note and attach it to the cartoon before presenting it to the person whose contribution you appreciate.

***

Never underestimate the value of happy face stickers.

***

Provide "shareable" recognition—a pizza, a box of doughnuts, or another treat—so that the recipient can share with other team members who helped complete a project.

***

Just Like at the Olympics:
- Create a poster featuring a gold medal or the medal podium. Under the heading "Gold Medal Performers," list all members of the team.
- Highlight the team's successes with a ceremony to present gold medals to team members. Create a simple medal with pieces of ribbon and a chocolate coin wrapped in gold foil.

***

Recognition That Takes Flight: This technique literally rises above others. Write your message on a sheet of paper before folding it to form a paper airplane. Launch it in the direction of the person whose performance was recognition worthy.

Important? Certainly. But Recognition Can Be Fun, Too

Airborne staff recognition might really take off. Soon the air could fill with paper airplanes delivering messages acknowledging the contributions of colleagues, like a bunch of Amazon delivery drones.

***

Hold an "Innovative Idea Day." Challenge staff members to come up with ways to improve service, reduce red tape, save money, etc. Every idea is worth points that staff members can use to purchase items from an inventory of small prizes, treats, etc. Review the suggestions, identify ones that can be adopted, acknowledge the source and invite the people responsible to help implement them.

***

Provide a team that has successfully completed a project the budget to plan a team celebration.

***

Spell out a message of appreciation with Scrabble tiles.

***

Recognition as a Comic Strip: The first comic strip appeared in the *New York World* newspaper in 1895. You may not be a Charles Schultz or Scott Adams, but that doesn't mean that you can't draw a stickman cartoon strip to show how a staff member contributed in a way that was effective.

***

Create a Gumby Award (named after the green claymation humanoid figure that first appeared in 1953) for someone who demonstrates flexibility. (You should be able to find flexible Gumby figures in your local toy store or online.)

***

Babe Ruth Award (a toy baseball bat) for someone who isn't afraid to strike out when trying to hit one out of the park. (The "Bambino" struck out more than any other MLB player—1,330 times—on his way to recording 714 home runs.)

***

A Forrest Gump Award (box of chocolates) for a staff member who demonstrated calmness when dealing with the unexpected. "My mama always said, 'Life is like a box of chocolates. You never know what you're gonna get.'"

***

Dispense a PEZ candy from your superhero dispenser whenever someone does a "super" job.

***

At the end of the year, one school principal asks teachers to share their funniest/most embarrassing teacher memories of the year. "These stories lead to a good laugh and make everyone realize that they're not alone in their mistakes/failures."

***

Hold a five-minute dance party at the end of the day.

***

Small Gifts/Big Messages
- Rubik's Cube: To someone who solves a challenging puzzle.
- Magic 8 Ball: Thanks for your insight.
- Boomerang #1: Whenever there's a new idea, it always seems to come back to you.
- Boomerang #2: To welcome back a former ("boomerang") employee who is returning to the organization.
- Artist palette or a paint box: For someone who brings colourful [bright] ideas to the team.
- Toy off-road vehicle: For someone who is not afraid to follow the road less travelled.
- Clock: To someone who keeps to the schedule or is always on time.
- Cheese grater: To someone who contributed to the "grater" good of the company.
- Hammer: For helping us build a strong foundation.
- Plant: For helping us grow.
- Mirror: Your actions reflect well on our company.

Important? Certainly. But Recognition Can Be Fun, Too

- Kite: To someone who helped the organization reach new heights or whose performance soared.
- Lottery ticket: Your idea was a real winner.
- Glove filled with treats: For being there when an extra set of hands were needed.
- Desk lamp or flashlight: To someone who shone light on a problem that was holding us back.
- Toy train: To someone who helped the team stay on the right track.
- Toy frog: To a team member who helped us take a great leap forward.
- Stone: To someone you can always depend on, someone whose performance is rock solid.
- Star Wars toy: Your performance was out of this world.
- Stuffed toy giraffe: To someone who was willing to stick their neck out.
- Toolbox: To an individual who is always able to fix things when they go wrong.
- Toy rocket ship: To a staff member who launched an idea that really took off.
- Kaleidoscope: To someone whose contributions changed chaos into a thing of beauty.
- PEZ candy dispenser: To a staff member who dispenses great advice every time they open their mouth. Add to the impact of the award by selecting a dispenser in the image of the recipient's favourite cartoon character.
- Flower: To someone whose suggestion bloomed into something wonderful.
- Compass: You helped us find the right direction to move us forward.
- Paper fan: You have a fan!
- Sunglasses: Your performance was brilliant.
- A rattle: To someone who wasn't rattled on a day filled with unexpected events or requests.
- Spark plug: To a staff member who supplies the spark that gets things going.
- Light bulb: To someone who comes up with bright new ideas.
- A massage: To acknowledge someone's backbreaking work.
- Spatula: For doing a flipping good job!

Sweetening Staff Recognition

Candy shops are filled with treats that could be used to reinforce your words of appreciation:

Include a sweet treat (a chocolate bar, for example) with a quick note of thanks describing a specific way in which the individual has contributed.

***

Put out a bowl of candy for staff, with a note thanking them for their contributions.

***

There are companies from which you can purchase chocolate bars and other treats with wrappers bearing messages such as "Great Job!" or "Thanks for going ABCD (Above and Beyond the Call of Duty)." Keep a supply on hand so that you can express appreciation when the moment is right.

***

Use confections to convey your message of appreciation with humour:
- McDonald's gift cards: Thanks a billion. (The burger chain's slogan is "billions and billions served.")
- Hershey's Hugs: You deserve a hug
- Bottle of water: Thanks for helping us keep our heads above water
- Milky Way or Mars bar: For a performance that was out of this world
- Life Savers: For a person whose efforts saved the day. A real lifesaver!

> A bag of mints can be the starting points for umpteen humorous messages of appreciation:
> - You did a dyna-MINT job on that project
> - Thank you for your commit-MINT to the team's success
> - Your involve-MINT made a real difference
> - We really appreciate your excite-MINT about tackling this task
> - Your contribution today was worth a MINT to us

Important? Certainly. But Recognition Can Be Fun, Too

- Chocolate coins wrapped in gold foil: For the person who deserves bags of money
- Skor bar: We've been keeping score and you have helped make us winners. Or thanks for helping us score in a big way.
- Coca Cola: For an employee who is "the real thing" (a former Coke slogan)
- Excel gum: For the person who excelled at a task or did an excellent job on a project
- Extra gum: For someone who went the extra mile to complete a project
- Crunch bar: For someone who helped get us through another crunch time
- Mentos: Your contribution meant-oh so much to the project
- Easter eggs: You did an egg-cellent job
- Tea bag: Your contribution suited us to a T
- Bag of popcorn: This may sound corny, but we just wanted to pop by to say thank you for popping into action
- Soft drink: You're so-da-lightful

A Final Thought
A serious end to a section filled with fun ways to recognize staff:
- Humour can be risky. What some staff enjoy as a fun award may not be **Appropriate** for others. Know your staff.
- Humour based on ridicule or bullying has no place in staff recognition.
- Be aware that staff members for whom English is their second language may not understand humour that depends on puns for its effect and could take unintended offence.

Theme #15
A Year's Worth of Staff Recognition

Staff recognition knows no season and should never be limited to specific dates on the calendar. Staff members' contributions and what they achieve—both big and small—should be acknowledged as they occur. Recognition should be part of your daily routine, a constant in the workplace throughout the year.

That said, there are still ways to recognize staff that are better suited to certain times of the year. There are designated days and weeks that serve as reminders to celebrate the contributions of certain individuals or specific groups, or hint at ways in which individuals and team members could be recognized.[4]

Plan for a Year's Worth of Recognition

Assemble a calendar of opportunities to celebrate individual or team contributions and achievements: staff members' birthdays, service anniversaries and the many designated days, weeks and months throughout the year that mark special occasions or celebrate different professions, interests and foods. Identify those that relate to your organization and its purpose, or which could be opportunities to celebrate individual or team contributions and achievements.

---

4   The National Day Calendar (https://nationaldaycalendar.com/) lists hundreds of designated dates, weeks and months each year, some of which you may be able to link to staff recognition.

Create your own designated days or weeks to celebrate the contributions of individual staff members and teams. On "Jill Smith Day" (This could be on Jill's birthday, her service anniversary or a day selected randomly), encourage other staff to express why they appreciate the opportunity to work with Jill and how she contributes and what she achieves. During "Custodian Appreciation Week" celebrate the contributions of those who come in after hours to clean the workplace.

Add other dates, such as the anniversary of some of the team's significant achievements—completing a major project, reaching an important safety goal, or implementing a process to improve the customers' experience. Recalling successes shows that you remember the effort that went into those accomplishments and still appreciate what the team (or individuals) did.

Springtime, when Recognition Blossoms

Here are staff recognition tips for spring (March, April and May):

Express appreciation with a bedding plant that the recipient can plant in their garden.

***

On one of the first warm days of spring, allow staff to leave early to enjoy the sunshine.

***

Spring is graduation time. Write a note to offspring of staff members who are graduating. Congratulate them on a job well done. Express your wish for their future success.

***

There is an abundance of designated days and weeks during the spring months that can easily be incorporated into your staff recognition plans. Take advantage of these well-known annual observations to inject extra recognition into the workplace:

> "We give substitute teachers an Easter basket filled with goodies and the fixings for an Easter dinner. We also put in a nice note showing our appreciation."
>
> – School principal

The first Friday of March is Employee Appreciation Day. On this day, leaders are encouraged to recognize staff for how they contribute and what they achieve on the job—just as they should on all the other days of the year.

"I'm a big advocate of using recognition on a daily basis," says Bob Nelson, the author of several books about recognizing and rewarding employees and the person responsible for establishing Employee Appreciation Day. "But I did want to have one day where we could call attention to the topic and have conversations about its importance."

So go ahead and celebrate Employee Appreciation Day. Then, keep the recognition flowing the next week (and during all the weeks that follow) by taking time every day to acknowledge those who contribute to your organization's success.

***

On National Tartan Day (April 6) celebrate a trait considered a Scottish stereotype—being thrifty. Recognize employees who devise ways to save your organization a few dollars, or more.

***

With the world observing Earth Day on April 22, it's an ideal time to reflect on the ways individuals are contributing to your organization becoming more environmentally conscious. It's also a suitable time to consider how to make your recognition practices more eco-friendly. See Theme #18: Staff Recognition Goes Green (p 102).

***

When it comes time to celebrate Administrative Professionals Week (last full week of April) or National Administrative Professionals Day (on the Wednesday of that week), managers often fall into the trap of the "Three Fs" of staff recognition—food, flowers or fudge (and other sweet treats). Exercise a bit more creativity. Rather than taking your support staff to lunch, buying them flowers or delivering sweet treats, surprise them by doing something different, something that reflects their recognition preferences and interests.

***

On International Astronomy Day (the Saturday just prior to the first quarter moon between mid-April and mid-May), ask, "Whose performance is out of this world?"

***

On the last workday prior to Mother's Day (the second Sunday of May), offer the mothers on your staff "early dismissal" to allow them to be home to greet their children when they get home from school. See Theme #13: Include Family Members in Your Staff Recognition Plans (p. 71) for more suggestions of how to incorporate Mother's Day into your staff recognition plans.

***

The second Wednesday of May is National Receptionists Day, which is a reminder to thank those staff members who create a positive first impression of your organization, whether they are answering the phone or greeting visitors.

***

International Virtual Assistants Day is the third Friday of May. While they may never come into your office and could live down the street, across town or halfway around the world, virtual assistants are essential to the success of numerous organizations. Thank them regularly for what they do.

Recognition for a Summer's Day

Here are staff recognition tips for summer (June, July and August):

On a hot summer day, drop by every workstation with an ice cream treat (By the way, July is designated as National Ice Cream month).

***

If staff members are required to work outdoors on sizzling summer days, let them know they are appreciated by showing up with a cooler filled with cold drinks—non-alcoholic, of course; it's a workday!

***

Deliver a basket to a staff member's desk, filled with enough of their favourite foods that they can invite a colleague or family member to join them for a picnic during an extended lunch break.

***

On a warm day, thank staff for all their work indoors by inviting them to enjoy a break outdoors—away from phones and computer screens. Provide cold drinks.

***

Bring in ice cream and everything needed to build delicious sundaes for an unscheduled celebration of team success.

***

Create an outdoor break area with picnic tables where office staff can gather during coffee and lunch breaks. They might also gather there for meetings, free from PowerPoint slides.

***

Roll a barbecue onto your parking lot, don an apron and grill up burgers (or veggie dogs) at lunchtime. Or anytime during the year, welcome staff with breakfast that you prepare for them.

***

Students look forward to an early dismissal day. You can't do it every week, but what about allowing staff to leave early on a beautiful summer afternoon?

***

Give a staff member a novel by an author they enjoy or one in a favourite genre, to read in their backyard, at the beach or while on vacation.

***

Give staff the option to come in early so they can leave early to enjoy the sunshine, if doing so will not interfere with your operations. Be flexible. This option may not appeal to all due to its potential to disrupt family routine.

***

Offer an extended break on a warm, sunny afternoon and encourage staff to go for a walk or to just get outside to enjoy the fine weather.

***

Schedule a visit by a gourmet food truck and treat everyone to lunch.

***

Allow staff members to leave early to get a head start on their weekend—especially a long weekend (weather and workloads permitting).

Let Recognition Fall Like Autumn Leaves

Here are staff recognition tips for fall (September, October and November):

Fall is when students head back to school, which makes it an apropos time to focus on the learning needs of staff. Is there specific training or a course that would help staff members grow in their jobs or prepare them for their next career move (hopefully, within your organization)? Offering training that will help staff grow demonstrates that you value staff members and are pleased with their performance.

***

Keeping with the back-to-school theme, you can acknowledge the team's contributions and achievements with a special training event or a team-building activity.

> **Some Dates to Add to Your Fall Staff Recognition Calendar:**
> - World Teacher Day (October 5)
> - During Customer Service Week (First week of October), recognize staff members who deliver the type of service you wish your customers to receive.
> - Have a veteran on staff? Around November 11 (Remembrance Day in Canada and Veterans Day in the United States), thank them for their service to their nation.

***

Fall is when parents stock up on school supplies—pencils, pens, notebooks, etc.—before children return to school. Prepare your staff for the next few months with the tools they need to recognize their peers—thank-you cards, sticky notes, peer recognition tips, etc. Check out Theme #20: Recognition for Everyone: Unleashing the Power of Peer Recognition: Part B How Staff Members Can Recognize Their Peers (p. 118).

***

If you live somewhere where Daylight Saving Time ends the first Sunday of November, think of this as a gift of an extra hour to write notes of appreciation to staff, rather than an opportunity to grab an extra hour of sleep.

***

Thanksgiving Day Thoughts:

- Is there any holiday that could be more strongly associated with staff recognition than Thanksgiving Day? When you think about your staff, who are you thankful for? Why? Let them know with a simple note or during a conversation.
- Saying thank you is so important. So why not celebrate Thanksgiving twice? Canadian Thanksgiving is the second Monday of October and American Thanksgiving, the fourth Thursday of November.
- While the fourth Thursday of November is American Thanksgiving, it's just another Canadian workday. But you can make it special by declaring it "Thank-You Thursday" in your workplace. It may work so well that you might want to observe Thank-You Thursday once a month—or every week.
- On the days around Thanksgiving, end emails to staff members with "Happy Thanksgiving." Add a postscript that begins, "What I am thankful for is . . ." and conclude with a specific description of what the recipient did that you appreciate:
    - ". . . the opportunity to collaborate with you on [project X]."
    - ". . . how you helped your colleagues complete the month-end report in record time."
    - ". . . the way you, Joyce and Ali pitched in to organize our potluck."

The more specific your description of what the person did, the stronger your message of appreciation.

Recognition that Removes Winter's Chill

Here are staff recognition tips for winter (December, January and February):

On a chilly winter morning, greet people as they arrive with a steaming mug of hot chocolate.

***

With every holiday card you write to staff members, express appreciation for at least one contribution the individual made during the past year.

***

Create an Advent calendar of gratitude. Each day during December, open a door to expose a message expressing gratitude to an individual or team.

***

'Tis the season of school concerts. Provide opportunities for parents to leave work to attend their children's daytime performances.

***

Personally deliver candy canes (or another sweet treat) to everyone's workstation, along with an **Explicit** description of something that the person did that you appreciate.

***

What challenges did your organization face during the past year? How were they overcome? Remind the people who helped address these issues that you know and remember what they did by thanking them again.

***

At year-end, reflect on your team's list of accomplishments since January. Trace specific successes to the efforts of one person or to a group of employees, if possible, to ensure that their contributions are acknowledged.

***

Help prepare staff to set New Year's resolutions by asking, "Where do you see your career in five years? What steps can you take during the next 12 months that will help you get there? How could I help you move closer to your career goals?" Check out Theme #10: Linking Staff Recognition to Career Goals (p 59).

***

Retail stores and offices may be closed on Christmas Day so that staff can spend time with their families, but there are organizations for which December 25 is just like any other day. There is no pause button they can push just because it is Christmas. Police, health-care workers and firefighters are the first that come to mind, but there are scores of other organizations that operate 24/7, 365 days a year—hotels, restaurants, utility companies, media organizations, etc.

If you are a supervisor or manager who has the day off but there are others who must work or be on-call during the holiday, take a moment to think about them. Sure, they may receive extra pay, but money isn't everything. Let them know that you appreciate them sacrificing time with family and friends. Think particularly about those who volunteer to work on a holiday so that co-workers can spend time with their families. Send them a text or email expressing your appreciation. Give them a phone call or drop in for a few minutes to express appreciation in person. Arrange for them to receive a special treat during their break.

***

If you don't work for an organization that operates 24/7 during the holidays, think of those who are required to be on duty. Take time from your celebrations to drop off a special treat to them.

***

End the year with a message to every staff member. Describe what you value most about having had them on the team over the past year. Focus on the individual's contributions to the organization as well as on what their work team achieved. Finding contributions to highlight will be easier than you think. When you sit down to write your emails, you will discover that two or three contributions jump out for each person. Don't be surprised if you hear from some staff members that you have given them the "best Christmas gift ever from a manager or employer."

Recognition that Removes Winter's Chill

***

Have you ever wondered how many letters Santa Claus receives each January? From Halloween to Christmas Eve, children send him lists of the toys, books and games they would like to find under the tree. What happens after Christmas? Not much. His mailbox is quite empty after December 25—nothing there but a bunch of bills. Few children thank Santa for the gifts he delivered. Encourage the children in your home to spend part of the holiday season expressing gratitude for what they received. Santa would certainly appreciate hearing from them—and you will be contributing to building a future generation of leaders who will know how to say thank you and how to recognize those with whom they will work.

***

During the holiday season, think of others. Your family and friends, of course, but also the people who deliver your mail or newspaper and pick up your garbage and recycling. And there are those who are less fortunate. Donate to charities, support your local food bank, etc.

***

Avoid missing key dates in staff members' lives, such as service anniversaries and birthdays, by entering them in your calendar at the beginning of the year.

***

Express gratitude by brushing snow off a co-worker's vehicle at the end of the day.

***

In January, start preparing to celebrate what will happen over the next twelve months with a yearbook that will record the success story of

Staff Recognition Resolutions for a New Year:
- Resolve to express your confidence in staff members with recognition that is sincere, specific, timely and personalized
- Resolve to read one book about staff recognition to discover new tools and techniques to express appreciation. Find new ways to recognize staff that you can adopt or adapt.
- Resolve to schedule time during the new year to step back and assess your staff recognition efforts and adjust if necessary

Note: There's no need to wait until the new year to resolve to provide more recognition. Do it now! You can always adjust your plan in January.

your organization and staff. Throughout the year, gather examples of what individuals and the team achieve and how they contribute to the organization's success. Collect media coverage and positive notes from customers (remember to also provide copies to the individuals that customers identify as exceptional, as you receive them). Take photos of employees at work. Record key events and milestones as they occur during the year, noting the employees responsible for these specific successes. Capture information on new hires, retirements and significant service anniversaries. Bring all this information together in a yearbook you unveil at a year-end celebration. Then begin collecting next year's moments to remember and celebrate. Create a tradition of celebratory yearbooks in your organization.

***

Observe National Handwriting Day (January 23) by writing thank-you notes to members of your staff.

***

Some of your staff members may have set New Year's resolutions but we all know how few resolutions are ever realized. While some pledges will be personal (i.e. none of your business), others may be work focused. How can you support their efforts to grow and improve? Could you offer them the opportunity to take relevant courses? Do they need a mentor or a chance to job shadow someone? By offering support, you demonstrate that you know and care about staff members as individuals.

***

A Final Thought
Year-end is a smart time to review your staff recognition practices. Think back on what you did to recognize staff over the past year. What worked? What didn't? What staff recognition techniques appear less effective? What worked for some staff members but not others? Have you recognized staff frequently enough? How could you improve your staff recognition practices? Use what you learn to improve your staff recognition plan for the new year.

Theme #16
Add Meaning to Formal Recognition

Too often, recognition is erroneously equated with programs that formally celebrate employees for reaching specific service anniversaries, achieving significant outcomes, or being designated as an employee-of-the-month. Typically, these recognition programs are governed by an abundance of rules to ensure "fairness" and feature costly events and expensive gifts for those being recognized.

Due to the expense and time involved in planning and hosting formal employee recognition events, the number of individuals recognized is limited and overall recognition is infrequent. Formal staff recognition events are often hosted away from the workplace and away from those with whom the recipients work, who know and care about them. No doubt, many appreciate being feted at big recognition events and receiving expensive gifts to mark certain service anniversaries, but there is little evidence that formal staff recognition programs have any impact on staff morale, engagement or retention.

Few employees ever said, "I stay because my employer did such a terrific job of celebrating my five years of service," but many initiated a job search because they felt their boss didn't show appreciation regularly for what they did.

This book is not about how to organize formal employee recognition events or the best awards to present after five or ten years of service. But formal recognition programs and events do exist and there are inexpensive ways to build on those programs to make what happens more meaningful for the recipients:

When staff members receive awards, ensure that their co-workers know. Announce their names to the others on the team. Schedule time to celebrate the award with the recipients' co-workers.

Thanks, Again!

***

Include information about award recipients in your external newsletter, on your website and in media releases.

***

Always attend events at which members of your staff are being recognized. Failing to do so, even if you have a busy schedule, is easily misinterpreted as you not caring.

***

Take photos at recognition events and post them on bulletin boards, on social media, or on a website where others will see them.

***

Have co-workers sign a certificate or work-related artifact (an apron in a restaurant, hockey stick in a sporting goods store, etc.) to mark the occasion.

***

Prior to a staff member's employment anniversary, invite everyone in the department to submit a congratulatory message, poem or a memento that underscores the event. Collect what they provide and present that on the staff member's anniversary.

> **ABCD.**
>
> These letters reflect what is often the essence of formal staff recognition programs, which have as their purpose rewarding those who go, "Above and Beyond the Call of Duty." This sounds like a noble goal, but what does it mean and who does it exclude? Certainly, staff members who do outstanding work deserve to be recognized. But there are others who seldom rise to this ill-defined level of performance. They are the people who arrive on time every day and go about doing their jobs as required for the organization to succeed. Their proficiency creates a platform from which others launch their ABCD-quality performances. Formal recognition programs lack a **DTJWED** category for those who **Doing The Job Well Every Day.** That's where informal, day-to-day recognition becomes essential—more important than formal recognition. Providing high-value, low-cost staff recognition touches more people, more often than formal recognition programs can ever hope to do.

***

Add Meaning to Formal Recognition

Highlight how the career of the recipient has developed and what they have achieved since their last service anniversary. Invite co-workers to describe how the individual has had an impact on them and their work experience.

***

Send a congratulatory note to the recipient's home

***

If your recognition program requires a supervisor's approval before recognition is bestowed, ensure that the timeline for approval is short to ensure the recognition is **Timely**.

***

Be creative when choosing the venue for your formal recognition event. Skip the hotel banquet rooms in favour of less traditional locations, such as an aquarium or zoo, science museum, art gallery or private room at a sports stadium.

***

Certificates can be an effective staff recognition tool when they capture the uniqueness of what each person contributes.

A certificate that congratulates Jordan for "his significant contributions to the ABC project" that is just like the one all his colleagues received has less meaning than a document that refers to two or three specific ways that Jordan contributed to the project's success. Prepare unique lists for each team member's certificate.

***

Formal celebrations-of-service events can feel impersonal. Rather than waiting for the next once-a-year event, acknowledge each staff member on, or as close as possible to, the actual anniversary of their start date. It is more personal and will be more appreciated by staff members.

***

When acknowledging service anniversaries, strengthen your message of appreciation by referring to which anniversary is being celebrated—the third, ninth or twelfth. This makes it the recipient's anniversary, not "anybody's" anniversary.

***

Consider holding a recognition event—not one of those big events with lots of speeches and only a handful of people being recognized—but a low-key celebration at a regular meeting or during a staff retreat. Prepare by identifying one trait you appreciate for each staff member. How is it reflected in what the recipient does, and why is it important to the organization? During your presentation, highlight the value of each staff member to the organization.

***

Follow up staff recognition events with a three-question assessment:
- What went well?
- What could have been done differently?
- What was the one key lesson we learned that could apply to staff recognition events in the future?

***

A Final Thought
Formal staff recognition programs cannot stand alone. They need to build on the foundation of a strong culture of appreciation and be rooted in informal, day-to-day recognition that staff members value. If expressing gratitude is not part of the workplace culture, formal staff recognition programs have little chance of success.

Theme 17
The Gift of Time

Time is a finite resource—both your time and that of your staff. This makes time the most valuable resource in your staff recognition tool kit. The more of this valuable resource you share with them, the more they will believe that you value them as people and appreciate them for what they do:

Just sharing a bit of your day with a staff member demonstrates that you value staff members as individuals. There are different strategies to being accessible. Schedule office hours or times when you will be available to take calls from staff. Plan regular one-on-one meetings with staff members. Put up a "Do Not Disturb" sign. Turn off your cellphone. Maintain neutral facial expressions and body language. Resist the temptation to offer solutions or rebut what others say. You're there to listen, so listen!

***

Surprise a staff member by offering to assume their duties while they take an unexpected hour off.

***

Spending time in the break room or visiting individuals at their workstation is a way of showing you value and appreciate staff members, but only if you are truly in the moment. Give staff your full attention. Listen to what they are saying. No multi-tasking!

***

Make the weekend special for members of your team by committing to not sending them work-related emails or text messages until Monday morning.

***

Everyone loves being able to leave early. It's something you can let them do occasionally, but never without linking this reward to a contribution or achievement. Otherwise, leaving early becomes a perk to which staff will soon feel entitled. Be specific in describing why you have decided staff deserves the opportunity to leave early. What contribution or achievement are you celebrating?

***

Say thank you to team members by telling them to take a longer lunch or to extend a break. Or allow them to leave early or come in later one day.

***

Do all—or most—staff members take their breaks at the same time? If so, that's when you should take your break. Being in a break room when everyone is there gives you the opportunity to listen to what staff is saying—what's happening, their frustrations and challenges and what's going well. What you hear may point to opportunities to acknowledge contributions. Tuck away what you learn so that you can recognize staff later—but not too much later.

***

Hold staff meetings only when you must. If no agenda items require immediate action, cancel the meeting.

***

> *"Show respect for staff members' time by scheduling division or department meetings, rather than all-staff meetings. These meetings are shorter for participants and contain only topics most relevant to them. More staff members will get to speak. They will get more attention from their supervisor. It builds, shares and rewards teacher leadership."*
>
> – Anonymous program participant

***

Schedule a one-on-one lunch with a staff member who made an important contribution to a recently completed project. This will work best if you know the staff member well enough to focus the conversation on your guest's interests and if you dine in a restaurant that serves food that your guest enjoys, whether it's burgers or seafood, Chinese or vegetarian.

***

A Final Thought
Just taking a moment to talk—and listen—makes staff members feel valued. On a staff list, note every time you speak to each person. Keep the gap between conversations short.

Theme #18
Staff Recognition Goes Green

Are your staff recognition practices environmentally friendly?

Staff recognition practices can be unfriendly to the environment, especially when managers and supervisors rely on certificates, plaques, trophies and trinkets that recipients don't value and will never use. Even staff members who were grateful for a certain gift previously may now feel they have enough of them. What once might have been treasured becomes a wasted gesture, destined for the recycling bin or landfill.

Before you present another certificate or desk clock, consider the alternatives:

Say thanks in person, with a smile and a firm handshake or a pat on the back.

***

Know your staff well enough to ensure that the recognition is **Appropriate**. Do they like to receive certificates, small gifts or thank-you notes? If not, find other ways to express your gratitude—a pat on the back, a mention in the company's newsletter or on the website, or a gift card to their favourite coffee shop.

***

Wrap gifts in recycled paper.

***

Don't buy printed copies of books about staff recognition. Buy e-books. Encourage your public library to buy a print copy—then you and several others can borrow it. If you do buy a book, pass it on to a colleague after you finish with it.

***

Help save a tree and make recognition **Timely** by sending e-cards. Your message of appreciation will arrive the recipient's inbox immediately.

***

"I've been told that looking at nature is very good for people (it's calming, etc.), so I like to give plants and flowers to staff."

– Anonymous seminar participant

Present staff members with a plant to green-up their workplace and serve as a permanent reminder of your appreciation.

***

British and Dutch researchers found that having office plants created a better work environment. Why? One possible explanation is that greenery increases engagement by making people more physically, cognitively and emotionally involved in their jobs.

***

A Final Thought
There is nothing environmentally unfriendly about giving someone something that they will value and keep, which can make well-written thank-you cards an environmentally friendly way to acknowledge individuals for contributions. Some recipients will treasure them for years.

Theme #19
Assessing Your Staff Recognition Practices

Continuing to use the same recognition tools and techniques is fine if they are still working. But are they? Or are you in a recognition rut?

Research by OC Tanner suggests that many organizations are. In its 2021 Global Cultural Report it notes that, "87 per cent of employees say their organization's (recognition) program is stale, outdated, or used as disguised compensation."

Pause regularly to assess your staff recognition practices. What's working, and what's not? Observe how recipients react to the recognition you provide. Ask for feedback.

Use what you learn to tweak your staff recognition practices. Has the time come to abandon practices that have become stale or simply aren't working? Find out:

Invite feedback on your staff recognition practices from individuals and the team, both in person and via surveys. How am I doing? How could I do a better job of recognizing staff? What do you want more or less of? Do you believe the recognition you have received has been appropriate for you? What other types of recognition would you like to receive? What's missing from my staff recognition practices? How could we increase recognition in the workplace? Use the feedback you receive to improve how you recognize staff. Adopt or adapt practices you have read or heard about.

***

Here are two questions to help you learn whether staff members feel they are being recognized for the right reasons. "What do you do that I'm not noticing? Are your colleagues doing things that I am not recognizing them for, but I should be?"

***

Consider how often you are recognizing staff. "Do I need to increase/decrease the amount of recognition I provide?"

***

Reflect on who you recognized recently and why. "Who have I missed? Who should I focus on finding a reason to recognize?"

***

Are you recognizing staff as often as you feel you should? Perhaps your busy workload has pushed staff recognition aside. The solution may be to schedule a few minutes each day to express appreciation to those whose contributions you appreciate. Block time in your daily calendar to focus on positives. The recipients of your praise will feel good—and so will you.

> **Friday Questions**
>
> Wrap up your work week, whether it ends on Friday or on another day, by asking yourself:
> - Has the recognition I delivered this week been **GREAT**: Genuine, Relevant, Explicit, Appropriate and Timely?
> - Did I recognize staff for **Relevant** reasons (actions that reflect the organization's values or help achieve its goals)? What impact is recognition having on staff performance? Am I seeing more of the behaviours I want to see?
> - What worked? Which one or two gestures of appreciation stood out this week as effective or as something the recipients found meaningful?
> - Given the benefit of hindsight, were there any messages of appreciation that would have been more meaningful if they had been delivered differently? What could have worked better?
> - Is there an important contribution that has gone unrecognized this week? If there is, act now, before your week is over, to recognize those responsible.

***

Does staff respond positively to the recognition you provide? If they do, congratulations! You're doing an excellent job of recognizing staff. You are providing the type of recognition they value. But are any of your staff recognition practices outdated? Be vigilant for signs that techniques you use to recognize staff may have passed their "best before" date. Give those methods a break and find new ways to express appreciation when people do their jobs well.

***

Include questions about recognition during exit and stay interviews.

***

At least once a year, survey staff about recognition. Include questions on your annual staff survey. Better yet, use pulse surveys—brief, more frequent surveys that consist of as few as a single question—to gather feedback.

***

For a week, keep a daily log of who you recognized, how and why. At the end of the week, review your log. How well did you do? How many people did you recognize? Was the recognition **Appropriate** to each recipient? Were your descriptions of what they did **Explicit**? Did you make recognition **Relevant** by linking why you are praising them to one of your organization's values? Was the recognition **Timely**? What small improvement can you make next week to how you recognize staff? (Repeat this exercise regularly.)

***

Assemble focus groups of staff members to provide feedback on how staff recognition occurs. It may be best to invite an outsider to facilitate these focus groups. Some may be reluctant to express their true feelings if you are the one leading the discussion. You can work with the facilitator to identify topics on which you want feedback: frequency of recognition, how contributions are recognized, what's being recognized and what's being missed, whether they feel cared for as individuals and appreciated for what they do. Do they feel they are where they belong?

***

Pause regularly to ask yourself: Am I recognizing individuals, or am I relying on team recognition? Both are important, depending on the nature of the contribution or achievement.

***

If your organization has a formal staff recognition program, is it still meeting the purpose for which it was established? Does anyone remember why the program was created? Is your recognition program up to date? Some programs are based on values that were retired years ago. It's time to reconsider the program. Is there a better way to express appreciation?

***

Some tokens used to express appreciation become tired over time, but here is a way you can breathe new life into one approach that might be worn out. Go beyond simply engraving the company logo on the side of a travel mug. Add specific words of appreciation or a carefully selected quotation that would be meaningful to the recipient. Avoid the trite teamwork-related cliches found so often in workplaces: e.g. Together Everyone Achieves More, or There's no I in TEAM. Quote a business guru or world leader that the recipient admires, or one of their favourite authors. Select a quotation that reflects their interests or hobbies. Or engrave a message from you to acknowledge the important achievement for which you are recognizing the individual. The more personalized the inscription, the greater the impact the message of appreciation delivers on your behalf, both when you make the presentation and with every sip.

***

To avoid staff recognition becoming hackneyed because you always say thank you in the same way, commit to discovering and implementing one new technique within the next 30 days.

***

A Final Thought
Reset your staff recognition goals frequently—at least once a year or even monthly. Adopt or adapt new tools and techniques and abandon those that have become less effective.

Surveys: How to Ask

There are two ways in which you can ask questions on surveys. The more common approach requires staff to respond to statements using a five-point Likert scale (Strongly disagree, Disagree, Neither agree nor disagree, Agree, Strongly agree) to statements similar to these:

- I receive meaningful recognition for doing my job well
- The recognition I receive aligns with the goals and values of the organization
- The recognition I receive focuses on what I must do to do my job well
- Recognition goes to individuals and groups when they deserve it

The advantage of asking questions in this way is that they can be answered quickly, which means that you can ask about several aspects of workplace life in one survey. On the other hand, this approach may produce results that are challenging to interpret, making it difficult to act without seeking more input.

For example, what does it mean if 40 per cent disagree and 40 per cent agree that they "receive meaningful recognition?" What are you to do?

An alternative approach is "gap research," which enables respondents to state how they perceive the workplace and how it could be improved. Four questions are asked about a topic.

Here's how the topic of receiving meaningful recognition could be explored using gap research:

1. On a nine-point scale, with nine high, how satisfied are you with recognition that you receive for doing your job well?

2. Why did you give this rating?

3. Knowing us as you do, if we really put our hearts into improving how we recognize staff, how satisfied could you be (using the same nine-point scale)?

4. What would we have to do to get there?

The first and third questions establish the gap between how respondents perceive the current situation and how they feel it could be. Question 2 invites respondent to explain why they rated the current situation as they did.

How staff answer question 4 is most important. By telling you in their own words what needs to change, staff members are contributing to a plan for improvement. Their words may become your action plan.

Section III
Responding to Staff Recognition Needs of Specific Groups

Peer recognition, remote workers, teams, diversity and inclusion and recognizing upward.

Theme #20
Recognition by Everyone: Unleashing the Power of Peer Recognition

Recognition doesn't have to be—and shouldn't be—the exclusive domain of people in leadership positions. Co-workers can be a potent source of meaningful recognition. Peer recognition increases the amount of recognition occurring within the workplace, which strengthens the culture of appreciation.

Peer-to-peer recognition is powerful. In fact, there may be no more meaningful recognition. No one knows better what a person does than the colleagues who work next to them and do the same or similar jobs. Because colleagues know what it takes to be successful, their praise of their peers has credibility.

Co-workers are there to witness others doing their jobs well, so the recognition they provide can be **Timely**. They can recognize co-workers instantly when they see behaviour that contributes to individual and organizational success.

Part A: How Leaders Can Encourage Peer Recognition

As a frontline leader, you can encourage recognition among peers in many ways:

Recognition is infectious. You will encourage peer recognition simply by conscientiously recognizing others, yourself. Become a role model, an example of what to do. The more often you express appreciation, the more likely it is that members of your team will heed your advice to express appreciation to their co-workers. They will begin to recognize the efforts and achievements of others more often.

***

Become a catalyst for peer recognition. During one-on-one meetings, ask questions:
- What was completed since our last meeting? (*The answer to this question may yield reasons for you to recognize the staff member.*)
- Which colleagues made your job easier? What did they do? (*Answers may expose reasons for the staff member to recognize a colleague.*)
- How did you/could you let this person know that you appreciated what she did?" (*The answer permits you to encourage peer recognition and to suggest ways they could recognize their peers.*)

***

Provide staff members with suggestions of ways to recognize their peers.[5]

***

Distribute thank-you cards at a staff meeting and encourage everyone to write at least one message of appreciation to a co-worker whose support and assistance they appreciate. Collect the cards and deliver them to staff

---

5 *Peer Recognition: Acknowledging Colleagues for What They Do* cards include several peer recognition suggestions and are available in the bookstore at www.GREATstaffrecogntion.com/

members' mailboxes. Let staff know where they can find more thank-you cards and encourage their use.

***

Establish an "Appreciation Station" and make it accessible to all staff, such as in the break room. There, staff can always find the tools they can use to express appreciation to colleagues, such as thank-you cards, sticky notes, etc. Don't worry if some thank-you cards are taken for personal use. Writing messages of appreciation to anyone is good practice.

***

Encourage staff members to recognize colleagues by having them enter their names into a draw for a weekly prize (lunch, coffee card, movie pass) when they recognize a co-worker's fine work or contribution with a thank-you note. Include entry slips in the cards that are available in the Appreciation Station.

***

Use an All-Star board in the staff room to honour a different staff member each week. Other staff members can use paper stars to describe their colleague's achievements and contributions and what they appreciate about them. Post these messages on the board.

***

Mission statements and values can languish in unread documents or on posters no one notices, or you can choose to bring them to life by encouraging stories of values in action. Create a display divided into sections, one for each of the organization's values (such as teamwork, integrity or customer service) where staff members can post descriptions of what co-workers do that illustrates the organization's values in action.

***

Invite staff to tell you when co-workers have been particularly helpful. Follow up with notes to let staff members know you are aware that they did well.

***

Observe Peer Recognition Day: A decade ago, in my first book, *Thanks! GREAT Job!*, I suggested designating the third Tuesday of each month as Peer Recognition Day. It's a day to remind staff to acknowledge their co-workers for what they do: helping create a positive work environment, assisting others complete their work, or contributing to the organization's success in other ways.

***

Publish a calendar of staff birthdays for the year (dates, but not years). The purpose here is not to remind staff to sing "Happy Birthday," but to use these milestones to create opportunities for staff to celebrate how their colleagues helped the company and their co-workers achieve their goals. Encourage staff members to thank the birthday celebrants for how they assisted them over the previous 12 months and to express their appreciation.

***

Encourage peer recognition by adding a postscript to the end of emails you send to staff members, reminding them to recognize colleagues. "Have you recognized a co-worker today for what they did to help or support you?"

***

Create a Pass-along Award: Use a new or repurposed trophy, a stuffed toy, or an item that reflects what your organization does as a symbol of success that staff members can pass to each other. Recipients become responsible for passing it along to another deserving co-worker within a few days.

***

Issue a peer recognition challenge: within 48 hours of being recognized themselves, staff members should find a reason to recognize a co-worker.

***

Set aside time at staff meetings for staff members to acknowledge the contributions of co-workers. Show the importance of recognition by scheduling this activity for early in the meetings, which is where the most significant topics should appear on an agenda. Prior to meetings, prime the pump by suggesting that staff members think of reasons to recognize co-workers to ensure they will arrive prepared to recognize others. Limit the time devoted to peer recognition to ensure that reasons to recognize colleagues are not exhausted before the time allocated for this activity expires. You never want to be in a position of begging for more peer recognition. Before moving on to the next topic on the agenda, acknowledge that there wasn't enough time to recognize everyone and encourage staff to recognize co-workers between meetings.

***

Recognize the recognizers. Encourage more peer recognition by praising staff members who recognize their colleagues.

***

Provide a budget and your support to allow staff to develop their own ways to say thank you to their colleagues.

***

Randomly assign one colleague to each staff member. Their assignment: to find a reason to recognize that person within the next week.

***

Write an article for your staff newsletter describing someone who does a splendid job of recognizing others.

***

Invite staff members to write brief descriptions of what a co-worker did that made a difference and include what they write in the staff newsletter.

***

> **A Final Thought**
> While peer recognition is powerful, it doesn't release managers from their responsibility to recognize staff. When the only recognition they receive comes from co-workers, staff will begin to believe that their leaders don't care about them or what they do. They will become less engaged; morale will decline and more people will decide that your workplace is not where they belong.

Part B: How Staff Members Can Recognize Their Peers

Wherever you are within the organization—on the front line or part of the leadership team—you are in a unique position to recognize your colleagues.

The recognition you provide to your peers makes a difference. Your recognition will resonate with your colleagues because they know that you understand what they do and know when they do their jobs well. Here are some ways to express appreciation to you colleagues:

When you succeed, thank those whose support and assistance helped you succeed—co-workers, people from other departments, a supplier, your supervisor or a family member.

***

Help keep the culture of recognition strong in your workplace. The next time you are recognized, pay it forward. Find a reason to recognize a colleague for a specific contribution or achievement within 24 hours. Keep the appreciation flowing.

***

When a colleague does a fantastic job, which you feel is deserving of recognition, tell your boss and encourage them to recognize your co-worker.

***

When you witness a staff member's recognition-worthy contribution, describe what they did on a card, sign it and have your boss sign it, too, before presenting it to the person.

***

Give credit to your team or co-workers. When you accomplish something worthwhile that catches the attention of others, accept their praise, but also mention how much others contributed to your success. When you give credit to others, they will continue to help you look good.

***

Part B: How Staff Members Can Recognize Their Peers

Here is the workplace equivalent to passing notes to classmates when you were in school. Slip a colleague a note of appreciation during a meeting. It will lift the meeting's mood and you don't have to worry about the teacher catching you.

***

During virtual meetings, use the chat feature of online meeting platforms to "pass" notes of appreciation to colleagues who work remotely.

***

Search for ways to help a colleague without being asked to, to say thank you.

***

Be the recognizer you want others to become. The more you recognize colleagues, the more likely they are to recognize others.

***

Headed for the break room or the local coffee shop? Offer to bring back a cup of coffee for a hard-working co-worker.

***

Picture a co-worker in your mind. What do you appreciate about this person? Make a list, then share it with your colleague.

***

Listen carefully when people recognize you. They are describing what they feel you did well, which is behaviour they value and want to see repeated. Accommodate them. Commit to continuing to perform in ways others value.

***

When you are the recipient of general praise (i.e. "You always do an excellent job."), ask the person for a specific example of what you did well. ("Exactly what did I do that pleased you?") Both of you will benefit from the answer. You will learn what another perceives as a strength and the other person will learn to be more **Explicit** when recognizing staff.

***

At the end of the week, list the people who helped you out or who made a contribution you appreciated. If you haven't already done so, share your appreciation before these people leave for the weekend.

***

Leave an awesome recommendation on a colleague's LinkedIn profile.

***

Send an all-staff email, describing what a colleague did that you appreciated.

***

Create a certificate to recognize a co-worker as your colleague of the day, week, month or year. Include an explanation of why you are presenting the award.

***

Write an anonymous note to another staff member, mentioning what they accomplished or something that you like about their work.

***

Refill the candy jar on a co-worker's desk. (You likely helped empty it.)

***

> **A Final Thought**
> **Advice on receiving recognition**
> The best response when someone recognizes you is a smile and two simple words, *"Thank you."* Nothing more is required. Don't protest that praise is unnecessary because you were "just doing your job," or that "anyone could have done the same thing." Maybe that's true. Anyone *could* have done it, but *you* did it. And your colleague appreciates what you did.

Theme #21
Recognition of Staff Who Work Remotely

During the COVID-19 pandemic, many people found themselves working from home for the first time. For others, working remotely was old hat. They had already chosen to work from home or in other non-traditional places, such as coffee shops, libraries or satellite offices. Before the pandemic, they represented only a small percentage of the total workforce but the number of people working remotely was growing. The pandemic accelerated that growth.

The opportunity for flexible work hours or to work off-site is among the most popular employment perks. Some people seek the freedom to work on a different schedule than those who are in the office everyday—early in the morning, late at night or on weekends. Avoiding the cost and time commitment of commuting and associated parking fees can be more valuable to them receiving a pay increase.

Many traditional staff recognition practices don't work for people who work remotely and get into the office infrequently. You can't simply drop by their desks to say, "Great job!" or involve them in spontaneous celebrations of team successes. Other approaches are required to make them feel valued as part of the team and appreciated for what they do:

Remote workers can miss out on the perks that staff working on-site routinely receive—company lunches, treats in the coffee room, the opportunity to leave early. Demonstrate that they are valued members of the team and not overlooked by arranging delivery of their favourite treats or sending a gift card so they can take a break at a coffee shop close to where they work. If practical, invite them to staff lunches and other events.

***

If remote workers visit the office occasionally to meet with colleagues, use these visits as opportunities to acknowledge their contributions and achievements. Schedule one-on-one meetings. Arrange time for them to socialize with on-site colleagues.

***

Encourage on-site staff to recognize their off-site peers. Remind them to thank their colleagues who work remotely and who they depend upon to do their jobs well.

***

Call staff members working from home just to express appreciation. Be **Explicit** about why you called. Emphasize that what they do is important and is appreciated. Cite examples.

***

You really can't beat face-to-face conversations, but when in-person meetings aren't possible with remote employees, teleconferencing may be the next best thing, utilizing any of several simple, inexpensive conferencing websites and apps.

***

Schedule virtual lunches with team members, during which you encourage them to share stories of how they and their co-workers contributed or what they achieved.

***

During virtual staff meetings, schedule time for staff to express appreciation to colleagues, as you would during in-person meetings.

***

During video meetings with staff members who work from home, observe what's on display behind them. The photos, trinkets and other items can be an indication of what's important to them and may provide clues for

Appropriate ways to recognize them. (Tip: To avoid focusing more on what's on display and not on the meeting's discussion, take a screenshot that you can search later for clues of what's important to your colleague.)

***

You could send an award when a staff member who works from home reaches a service anniversary, but the gesture would be more powerful if you personally deliver the award to the individual's home, especially if you can present it with family members present. Whether it's sent or delivered, accompany the award with specific descriptions of how the recipient contributes and why these contributions are important and appreciated.

***

When staff members are working from home, it may be easier to involve families in what you do to recognize staff virtually. "Is your family around? Please invite them to come into the room. I think they would like them to hear what I am going to say to you."

***

An advantage of virtual meetings is that it is easier for senior leaders to drop in for a few minutes than is the case during traditional meetings, because no travel time is involved. Invite them to join your virtual meetings to express appreciation. Prepare them by describing individual or team contributions. You might even suggest what they could say.

***

Schedule telephone one-on-one meetings with off-site staff at least once a month. Deal with the topics on your agenda, but leave sufficient time to acknowledge staff members for what they do and to discuss any questions, concerns or suggestions they have related to their work.

***

Ensure that folks working remotely have the resources they need to do their job, which are readily available in the traditional workplace. Provide them with an allowance to purchase the supplies they need to do the job.

***

Thanks, Again!

During the pandemic, we learned that people working from home can fail to establish boundaries between work and their personal lives. Some found themselves working more hours than their on-site colleagues. Working extra hours can create stress for staff members and their families. Remind staff working remotely to take care of themselves. Encourage them to take regular breaks, just as they would if they were in the office.

***

Never underestimate the impact it makes on an off-site staff member's day to receive a handwritten thank-you note in the mail.

***

Call off-site staff members on their birthdays with a few words about why you appreciate having them on your staff.

***

Your workplace is a community. Maintain that feeling by encouraging people to connect with each other, during virtual coffee breaks, for instance.

***

Express appreciation by extending opportunities for professional development through online courses or by providing how-to books that will enable working-at-home staff to learn new skills.

***

Be accessible to remote staff members. Schedule "office hours"—times when you will be available to take their calls.

***

If your travels take you near where they work, invite staff members working off-site to meet you for coffee or lunch.

***

Need reasons to recognize off-site staff? Ask them about what they consider their "recent wins." You may learn more about how remote staff contribute differently than on-site staff.

***

A concern of staff working remotely is that they will be overlooked for promotion. Ensure they are aware of promotion opportunities and assure them they will be considered. Working remotely should not cut anyone off from career advancement.

***

If remote staff members come into the office occasionally, try to schedule these visits to coincide with others' presence, to provide opportunities for them to meet face-to-face with colleagues—both others who work remotely and those who are regularly on-site.

***

How could working remotely be improved? Ask staff who work off-site for suggestions and consider how to implement them.

***

It could be easy to miss recognizing staff you don't see regularly. Keep off-site workers top of mind with a recognition log. Note times when you acknowledge their contributions and review this record regularly. How long has it been since you recognized each off-site worker? Is it time to find a reason to praise them for their efforts?

***

A Final Thought
When considering how to recognize staff working off-site, don't overlook what works for on-site staff. How could these practices be adapted to provide meaningful recognition to your remote workforce?

Theme #22
Diverse and Inclusive: Recognition for Workplaces Where All Feel They Belong

"Companies can mandate diversity, but they have to cultivate inclusion."

– Janet Stovall,
inclusion advocate (during a 2018 TED Talk)

As we watch, a duck appears to glide effortlessly across a peaceful lake. What we don't see is how furiously its feet are moving below the surface to maintain its forward motion.

This wilderness experience is similar to a workplace where diversity is obvious but where the demanding work that ensures its culture is inclusive is not easily seen or measured.

Creating a diverse workplace is the easy part. Creating and maintaining an inclusive workplace, where everyone feels they belong, is much harder. In *Birds of All Feathers,* Michael Bach uses the words of American diversity and inclusion consultant Steve Robbins to illustrate the difference: "Diversity has sometimes been about counting people. Inclusion is about making people count."

Recognition practices that are sensitive to the different experiences, values and beliefs of staff members is a way to ensure that people feel they count.

Diversity is metrics. It's about who is hired and about differences that are both visible (race, gender, age, disabilities) and invisible (religion, sexual orientation, family status).

Inclusion is about creating a workplace where everyone feels welcome and comfortable being themselves. In inclusive workplaces, everyone feels safe, valued and respected. Everyone is treated equitably. People feel they are where they belong and where they want to stay.

Research from 2017 by Deloitte found that 33 per cent of employees who left for workplaces with more inclusive cultures did not feel comfortable being themselves at their old workplace. Only 12 per cent reported leaving because the workplace did not have sufficient demographic diversity.

Bach writes that, "You can focus on the number of people you have from an underrepresented group, but if you don't focus on the bigger picture of ensuring those people feel included and valued, twice as many people from that underrepresented group will be going out the back door than coming in the front entrance."

At its core, inclusive staff recognition is about ensuring recognition practices are **Appropriate.** Inclusive recognition requires us to get to know and value the people we work with as individuals.

Unless inclusion is embedded in the workplace culture, attracting and retaining a diverse team will be difficult and perhaps impossible. A 2020 study by Glassdoor found the diversity of a workplace is a consideration of three quarters of jobseekers and is a crucial factor when evaluating companies and job offers, a figure that would be even higher were it not for the responses of white males. Here are some ways to build an inclusive workplace with staff recognition:

None of us are blind to race or gender, but all of us can see the person in front of us for who they are. Value people as individuals and recognize them for how they contribute and what they achieve.

***

Review your organization's values. Do they refer to diversity, inclusion and belonging? Do they need to be updated to support diversity and inclusion?

***

Respect and treat all staff members with dignity, without regard to their role within the organization. Everyone matters. Everyone contributes. Everyone has thoughts worth hearing.

***

Strive to understand the culture of others. Don't assume. Verify the truth about cultural stereotypes, which may introduce unconscious biases into your recognition practices. Ask questions to understand. "I want to learn more about you and your culture."

> **The Unequal Recognition of Men and Women**
>
> A study from Stanford University found that the praise women receive is different than that given to men. Managers tend to praise women with general, lukewarm language, while the recognition men receive is more specific: "57% of these generic comments went to women, while 43% went to men."
>
> Women were praised as helpers (doing "office housework, often called 'unpromotable work'") and men as leaders. "Whether it's conscious or not, we want women to care, but we want men to take charge."

***

Fear of offending others can prevent us from learning more about the values and culture of those with whom we work. What will they think? Will I be showing my ignorance? Will I be asking questions to which I should already know the answers? Don't allow fear and discomfort to stop you from asking people what you can do to ensure they feel they belong. If you don't engage with people, how will you increase your understanding?

***

Involve a diverse group of staff members in planning for recognition. Seek their input on how to celebrate success. Be prepared to change practices that may unintentionally exclude people (Family responsibilities may be a barrier to attending evening celebrations, events involving alcohol may deter the participation of others, etc.)

***

To avoid unconscious biases influencing how you recognize staff, identify three achievements or ways in which each staff members contributes. Be specific (**Explicit**) when recognizing them and why what they did matters (**Relevant**).

Diverse and Inclusive: Recognition for Workplaces Where All Feel They Belong

***

Names are important. Learn to pronounce ones that are unfamiliar. Ask staff members to assist you in mastering their name. Don't anglicize names to make it easier for you or expect staff to do so.

***

Determine which pronouns (he/she/they) staff members prefer and use them when referring to these individuals and encourage others to do the same.

***

Ask recent immigrants if they would like to acknowledge their national day.

***

Be aware of fun recognition that depends on puns for their effect, such as some found in Theme #14: Important? Certainly. But Recognition Can Be Fun, Too (p. 75). Staff members for whom English is their second language may not understand the humour and take unintended offence.

***

Ask questions about inclusion and belonging on staff surveys. Use what you learn to adjust your practices. (On a scale of one to nine, with nine high, how satisfied are you that our workplace is inclusive of people from different backgrounds? . . . that our workplace is somewhere where people from diverse backgrounds feel comfortable being themselves? . . . that our workplace is somewhere where everyone believes they belong?) See Theme #19: Assessing Your Staff Recognition Practices (p. 104) for more about conducting staff surveys.

***

Consider dietary restrictions when planning for celebrations that involve food. Avoid celebrations that involve food during times of religious fasting, such as during Ramadan.

***

Ask recent immigrants how to say "thank you" in their language. Use when appropriate.

***

Include questions about belonging in stay interviews:
- How successful have the leadership team and your co-workers been in making you feel welcome here? What else could we do?
- Do you feel comfortable that you can "be yourself" here? What could we do to make you feel more comfortable?
- How have the leadership team and your co-workers made you feel included here? What else could we do to help you feel that this is somewhere you belong?

For more on stay interviews, see Theme #8: Building Commitment from Day One (p.45).

***

People new to the country often want to learn about your culture as much as you should want to learn about theirs. They want to "fit in." Take time to explain cultural practices that they may find strange. Why do we do what we do? Encourage other staff to do the same. Make yours a workplace where everyone learns.

***

Some religions and cultures may forbid physical contact, including handshakes, between genders. As an alternative, follow the example of Muslim women, some of whom touch their hands to their heart when meeting people. It is a gesture we can all use. Symbolically, we are demonstrating that **Genuine** recognition comes from the heart, due to a sincere sense of appreciation for what the individual did.

***

Display a "Languages Spoken Here" sign that lists all the languages spoken by staff within your workplace.

***

Identify all languages that staff members speak on their name badges. This shows respect for their language skills and may prove useful when serving customers in their preferred language.

***

Provide badge and name plates with people's names in both English and their native language.

***

Make what you mail more inclusive with stamps issued by the post office to mark specific cultural observations (Lunar New Year, Black History Month, etc.) and significant religious celebrations (Eid, Hanukkah, Dawali, Christmas, etc.) Use these stamps on letters you send during these times of the year, especially when sending thank-you notes.

***

Establish "floater holidays" to enable staff members time to celebrate the religious holidays that are important to them.

***

Begin meetings with land acknowledgements that recognize that Indigenous people share their territory with those who came later as colonists or immigrants.[6]

> **Sample Land Acknowledgment:** I'd like to acknowledge that we are on Treaty 6 territory, a traditional meeting grounds, gathering place and travelling route to the Cree, Saulteaux, Blackfoot, Métis, Dene and Nakota Sioux. We acknowledge all the many First Nations, Métis and Inuit whose footsteps have marked these lands for centuries.

***

Everyone can contribute to developing a workplace culture of diversity and inclusion. Encourage peer recognition. Ensure all staff can give and receive recognition.

***

---

[6] For easy reference, here's a map of Canada's historical treaty territories: https://www.rcaanc-cirnac.gc.ca/DAM/DAM-CIRNAC-RCAANC/DAM-TAG/STAGING/texte-text/htoc_1100100032308_eng.pdf

Praise staff members who show their respect for the culture of others, demonstrate their support for inclusion or who help others feel they belong.

***

Who we are is shaped not by the colour of our skin or our gender, but by our background and experiences. Develop understanding by inviting staff members to share experiences that most define who they are.

***

Provide opportunities for staff members to share their cultures with co-workers. Michael Bach, the author of *Birds of All Feathers,* suggests beginning team meetings with a "diversity moment, when someone shares something about themselves to help educate their co-workers on the diversity that exists around them."

***

Monitor who is being recognized. Who is being excluded? Consider if any groups are left out by the nature of where and when they work (delivery drivers, custodial staff, warehouse workers, those working remotely, food service workers, etc.)—especially if the group includes people from different races, cultures or genders than the rest of the workforce.

***

When staff members come face-to-face with racist, xenophobic, homophobic, or misogynistic customers or co-workers, your role is to intervene, support and praise individuals for their professionalism is dealing with a difficult situation.

***

A Final Thought

The fear of doing the wrong thing can prevent us from doing the right thing. When dealing with people from diverse backgrounds we will make mistakes. That's OK, if our actions and questions are driven by a sincere hope to learn about the people with whom we work and a desire to create a workplace where all believe they belong. As with staff recognition, there is no endpoint for inclusion. There will always be more to learn, more to do.

"Do the best you can do until you know better. Then when you know better, do better."

— Maya Angelou, American writer

Theme #23
Recognize Bosses on Their Day—and All Year Long

"I have yet to find a man, however exalted his station, who did not do better work and put forth greater effort under a spirit of approval, than under a spirit of criticism."

– Charles Schwab, American businessperson

The need to be recognized never goes away, not even when someone is promoted. Managers, supervisors, principals, department heads and others in leadership positions need and deserve to be recognized from time to time. Just as leaders should let productive and engaged staff know they are valued and appreciated, staff should express gratitude to effective and supportive leaders.

National Boss Day—observed annually on October 16 (or on the nearest workday)—is a reminder to express appreciation for the boss's leadership and support. But it should not be just one day and done.

The need for recognition is no less important the day or a week after, or the day or a month before National Boss Day. Find ways to recognize your boss on National Boss Day and frequently throughout the year:

Have everyone sign a card for National Boss Day. Now that greeting card companies have discovered National Boss Day, you will be able to choose from assorted designs.

***

Skip the card shop and send the boss an environmentally friendly e-card—some are free, while others have a small fee associated with them.

***

Welcome the boss with a sign that proclaims, "Happy Boss Day!" signed by staff members. Some may wish to add words of appreciation.

***

Initiate a standing ovation for when the boss arrives for work or enters the department on October 16.

***

Leave a treat and a note of appreciation, saying thank you for the leadership the boss provides.

***

Organize a potluck lunch in the boss's honour.

***

Gather several small gifts to be delivered to the boss's desk throughout the day: coffee to start, a mid-morning treat, a gift card to his favourite retailer. End the day with a movie pass for the boss and a significant other.

***

Say thank you with the gift of an

> **Planning National Boss Day Recognition**
>
> Boss's Day originated in the United States in 1958 and is observed in several countries, including Canada. In 1979, Hallmark introduced its first National Boss Day cards. Here are a few considerations to have in mind as you prepare to thank your boss for the support and leadership you receive:
> - Check out the rules for gift-giving in your organization. Some companies and government agencies have policies that prohibit staff from accepting gifts.
> - It's better to work as a group to plan how to express appreciation to the boss. When only one or two individuals acknowledge the boss, it could easily be misinterpreted. The boss may wonder what you are expecting in return. Co-workers may believe you are trying to get into the boss's good books or question the nature of your relationship with the boss. Proceed only if everyone—or almost everyone—is on board. If others aren't interested in doing anything special, back off. You can still observe National Boss Day, but keep it low key.
> - Pass the hat among your co-workers to collect money to purchase a gift for the boss.
> - Keep gifts small. You don't want to dig too deeply into your colleagues' pockets. It's the gesture, not the gift's value, that's important. Choose a gift that relates to what's important to the boss, such as a book related to his hobby or favourite pastime, an opportunity to do something with the family, tickets to a sporting or theatre event, or a gift card to the boss's favourite restaurant.

appropriately illustrated calendar (after all, a new year will begin not long after National Boss Day). Choose a food calendar for someone who likes to cook, a hockey calendar for a sports fan, a calendar with photos of dogs or cats for a pet lover.

***

Purchase a book for the boss. It could be the latest management book, a new novel by their favourite author or a travel guide to a country that the boss dreams of visiting.

***

Invite the boss to join you and a few of your colleagues for lunch or coffee. Use this time to express gratitude for the boss's leadership. Allow the boss to choose the topics for the rest of the conversation. This is not a time to pursue your agenda.

***

Ask your co-workers to write messages for a gratitude book to present to the boss. Increase the number of positive messages by asking customers, your boss's boss and people from other departments to contribute their thoughts.

***

Create a package of coupons that the boss can exchange for lunch at the cafeteria, a cup of coffee delivered to his desk, fifteen minutes of unpaid overtime from an employee, a personal errand that a staff member will run during the lunch break, etc.

***

Google "leadership quotations." Select a few that capture the essence of your boss's leadership style and post them around the office.

***

Invite colleagues to complete the phrase, "What I appreciate most about [insert boss's name here] . . ." Type their comments (keep them anonymous if you wish), frame them and present them to the boss.

***

Have a travel mug engraved with a message of appreciation or an inspirational quotation. Fill it with a package of the boss's favourite tea or coffee or a coffee shop gift card.

***

Encourage your colleagues to fill the boss's inbox with positive email messages.

***

Tweet positives about the boss.

> **A Final Thought**
> If you supervise people who supervise others, remember to let them know that you appreciate them for the leadership they provide for their teams.

Theme #24
Team Recognition

Much of what is accomplished in the workplace is the result of people working together as a team. Celebrating how groups contribute to the organization's success strengthens team bonds and improves job satisfaction. Motivate people to achieve more as a team by recognizing what they achieve as a team:

Teamwork is a common organizational value, for good reason. When people work together, they can achieve more. But teams consist of individuals who may not always understand the importance of their unique contributions (and you may not either). Meet with team members individually to discuss how they contribute. Begin by asking, "How does what you do contribute to the team achieving success?" This is an opportunity for the staff members to describe how they feel they contribute.

Continue by asking, "Are there tasks you are asked to do that you feel don't support the team's goals? How could they be changed to make them more relevant? What other tasks could you take on that would make your contribution more significant to the goals of the team? How could we better use your strengths?"

Discuss these suggestions. Are they realistic? How could they be implemented?

***

When a team completes a project, acknowledge its success. Strengthen your message of appreciation by recognizing each individual for how they contributed to what the team accomplished. Because you are someone who allows a team to empower itself to complete tasks, you may not have first-hand knowledge of what each team member did. But the team leader will. Prepare yourself to supply individual recognition by asking the team leader for this information. Don't be shy about telling recipients about your research. "When I spoke to your team leader, she told me that you . . ." Include the team leader's description, followed by your thoughts about the value of those contributions.

***

If a team is assigned a project, recognize the whole team for its completion. Certain members may have contributed more than others and they should receive individual recognition. But recognize individual efforts away from the celebration of the team's success. Meet with individuals privately, before the team celebration, to acknowledge their specific contributions. They can then go to the team celebration knowing that you understand and value their individual contribution, as well as what the team carried out.

***

Celebrate a team's successful completion of a project by inviting an expert to make a presentation on a work or non-work-related topic selected by the team—personal health or fitness, golf, interior decorating, gardening, customer service, etc. Team members may be able to suggest someone with the expertise to make the presentation.

***

Recognize team success with a donation to a charity selected by the group or time off to volunteer with the charity.

***

Host a movie day to celebrate a team's success. Ask team members to choose the film they would like to see. Don't forget to supply plenty of popcorn and other treats.

***

Celebrate a team's success by ordering in lunch or by arranging for a special sweet treat during a break. You could give team members a change of venue and invite them to join you for an off-site lunch to celebrate.

***

If you schedule an on-site luncheon to express appreciation to the team, never leave early. Stick around to visit with staff. This shows that you believe the team is important and you want to spend time with them. Strengthen your expression of appreciation by being the one who stays to do the cleanup.

***

Invite team members to explain in their own words why the project they worked on was successful.

***

Celebrate team success with a departure from the routine. Hold a meeting in a different location. Rather than ordering pizza for lunch in the boardroom, host a celebratory lunch in a nearby restaurant. If circumstances permit, close the office—or reduce coverage to a skeleton crew—and invite everyone to join you for a matinee at a local movie theatre. Remember to do something special for the people who stayed back to hold down the fort.

***

Sharing a meal is always a wonderful way to celebrate a team success. You could take the team to a restaurant or have the meal catered. Even better, prepare the meal yourself. It may not match a professional chef's creation, but the time and effort you personally devoted to preparing the food will make your expression of gratitude stronger.

***

We all tend to have a preferred way to express appreciation, such as taking the team for lunch. This may be the type of recognition team members value. Or maybe not. Rather than assuming that your way to express appreciation is the best way to recognize the team, check how they feel about your plan. "I am thinking of taking you for lunch to thank you for completing this project on time and under budget. What do you think? Would you like to do that? Or is there a better way to celebrate your success?"

***

Display a photo of the team that just completed an important project, along with a description of what they did. Why was this project important to the organization? How and when did they complete the task? How did the team overcome obstacles it encountered? Did the team complete the task on schedule? On budget? What happened/will happen because of their efforts?

***

Begin a new project by reminding the team of its previous successes due to everyone working together.

***

Place an advertisement in a local newspaper that proclaims: "Here are 43 reasons that ABC Corporation is successful," followed by a list of everyone on the team—all 43 of them.

***

> **A Final Thought**
> Never lose sight of the fact that teams are made up of people, each of whom wants to be seen as an individual. Don't allow team recognition to push aside the recognition of individual staff members. Both are important. Team recognition does not diminish the need for individual recognition.

Section IV
Overcoming Barriers to Recognition

Challenges that threaten your staff recognition plans (no time, no money), staff recognition deniers and other barriers.

Theme #25
A Penny-Pincher's Guide to Staff Recognition

If you are like most frontline leaders, your budget for staff recognition is limited.

Worry not!

Costly gifts and trinkets and expensive events are not necessary to convey messages of appreciation. What makes staff feel valued and appreciated are your words—expressions of gratitude motivated by a **Genuine** sense of appreciation. **Appropriate** inexpensive trinkets, gifts and activities can strengthen that message:

Thank-you cards—Expensive when purchased in specialized card shops or from greeting card racks at pharmacies. Your nearest dollar store is a better option. There you'll find a variety of cards that look as good as what's in the more expensive shops for a dollar or so each.

Or head to the stationery departments of big-box stores, which sell cards in packages of ten to fifty, at prices that can be less than fifty cents per card. Buy several boxes, with a variety of designs, to avoid all your messages of appreciation looking the same.

***

Sticky notes—An even less expensive way to put your thoughts in writing. Even when you splurge and buy uniquely shaped or designed notes, each message you leave on a staff member's desk or attached to a computer screen will cost only a few cents.

***

Wall or desk calendars—They are **Appropriate** recognition when you find one that relates to the intended recipient's interests, whether it's travel, dogs, sports or fine art. These calendars are expensive, but you can save by waiting until after Christmas or a week into the new year, when stores—particularly those that pop up each fall—drop their prices. Discounts of up to 50 per cent are common and most recipients won't care if they receive your well-chosen gift in first weeks of the new year.

Another place to pick up low-cost calendars, even before the Christmas, is at wholesale stores such as Costco. Selection may be limited, but the prices are always discounted. They just might have the right calendar for a staff member whose contributions you appreciate.

***

Movie passes and gift cards—Pick these up at warehouse stores for less than face value. Some auto associations also offer movie passes that you can purchase at a discount if you are a member.

***

Loyalty program points—Assign points to others or use them to purchase an array of gifts that can help convey your message of appreciation.

***

Buy used—Here's your excuse to visit thrift and second-hand shops, used bookstores and garage sales. One person's trash may be the treasure that is right for one of your staff. Buy when you see it and then set it aside until the moment is right for you to recognize that staff member.

***

Conference swag—Conference attendees often receive a bag of goodies, the contents of which they will never use but which others might value. You may also have the opportunity to pick up other items when visiting trade show booths. Before you discard what you won't use, ask yourself: is there someone back at the office who would appreciate receiving this swag? Keep it until the next time you have an opportunity to recognize this person for a contribution or achievement.

∗∗∗

A Final Thought
Of course, the best way to keep costs down is to use low-cost, no-cost tools such as a few words of praise, a simple pat on the back or the gift of time. Even the opportunity to extend a break by ten or fifteen minutes or to leave a few minutes early at the end of the day can be a powerful way to reinforce your message of appreciation. For more suggestions of ways to use time as a staff recognition tool, see Theme #17: The Gift of Time (p. 99).

Theme #26
Staff Recognition Time Savers

Resources available for staff recognition—especially your time—are limited. But there are ways to work staff recognition into your already busy schedule:

How much time are you spending each week worrying about things over which you have no control? Stop doing that. Use the time to recognize staff members for how they contribute and what they achieve.

***

Always carry thank-you cards with you—in your purse or briefcase. Whenever you are waiting for an appointment or for a meeting to begin, use that time and your easily accessed cards to write notes to deserving staff members. For tips on using thank-you cards, see Theme #6: Staff Recognition's Number One Tool: Thank-You Notes (p. 39).

***

Take a moment at the end of the day or first thing in the morning to record a message of appreciation on staff members' voice mail. Hearing your words of appreciation first thing when they arrive for work will be a great start to their day.

***

Send text or email messages of praise during your commute (but not if you are the one driving!) or while watching television (better for your waistline than spending commercial breaks searching the refrigerator for snacks).

***

Short messages on sticky notes that can be stuck anywhere—desks, computer screens, letters from customers, etc. For more ways to use sticky notes as a staff recognition tool, see Theme #7: Recognition that Sticks (p 42).

***

On your way to and from your office, pause to express appreciation to individuals for their contributions.

***

Encourage Peer Recognition. When staff members acknowledge colleagues for what they do, it increases the amount of recognition everyone receives and enhances your culture of appreciation. See Theme #20: Recognition by Everyone: Unleashing the Power of Peer Recognition (p. 113) for ways you can encourage staff members to recognize their co-workers.

***

Write a note of appreciation on the back of your business card and leave it on the staff member's desk.

***

Use your smartphone to record brief video messages of appreciation to email or text to individuals or the whole team. Your message will be stronger when it's **Timely**, includes an **Explicit** description of what the individual or team did and shows how their deed is **Relevant** to the organization's goals, mission statement or values.

***

A Final Thought
Be prepared when it's time to recognize staff. Create a staff recognition tool kit and keep it nearby, so you don't have to spend time searching for what you need to thank staff members for what they do. For suggestions of what to include, see Theme #2: Filling Your Staff Recognition Tool Kit (p. 8).

Theme #27
How to Respond the Next Time Someone Says, "I Don't Recognize Staff Because . . ."

If you are reading this book, telling you about the value of staff recognition is like preaching to the choir. You already get it.

But not everyone does. There are managers and supervisors who don't understand the benefits of staff recognition. They don't believe staff recognition is important. You may know them. They rattle off a list of reasons for not recognizing staff. As a "believer," you see these reasons for what they are, just "excuses, rationalizations and cop-outs." But what can you say?

Excuse #1: I don't know how—Recognition begins with two simple words: thank you. Everything else you do to recognize staff is a refinement, just a different vehicle for conveying your message of appreciation. There are hundreds of simple, inexpensive ways to recognize staff.

Excuse #2: I don't have time—If you sincerely believe staff recognition is important, you will find the time because staff recognition need not take much time: a pat on the back, a few words of praise delivered in person, or with a handwritten note. By recognizing staff, you may actually save yourself time. People who feel valued and appreciated are more engaged and more engaged employees require less supervision. People are more likely to stay where they are appreciated—where they believe they belong. That improves staff retention and reduces the time you expend to recruit, interview and train new staff members. For tips on finding time to recognize staff, see Theme #26: Staff Recognition Timesavers (p. ##).

Excuse #3: I don't feel we should thank people just for doing their job—We cheer athletes and performers just for doing their jobs, don't we? We cheer them just for showing up for work (running onto the field or stepping onto the stage). And we cheer even louder when they do their jobs well, be it scoring a game-winning goal or performing their greatest hit. Why should it be different when your staff members meet expectations or perform well?

Excuse #4: I don't want to overdo it—It's hard to imagine that happening. While people regularly complain they aren't being recognized enough, no one ever complains about getting too much praise. The only caveat is that recognition becomes meaningless when it isn't deserved and the person doing the recognizing is only going through the motions. These attempts at recognition are not **Genuine**. True recognition means the person providing the recognition understands what the recipient did and why it was important.

Excuse #5: I don't want to miss someone—Hockey Hall of Famer Wayne Gretzky once said, "You miss 100 per cent of the shots you don't take." When you don't recognize anyone, you won't just miss someone, you will miss 100 per cent of the people who deserve recognition.

Excuse #6: I don't get any recognition myself—never have, didn't need it—This isn't about you, it's about the people with whom you work, who deserve and want to be recognized. Or maybe it is about you. What if you had received praise regularly? How would you have felt? What difference would that have made?

Excuse #7: It's not my job to recognize people—If not yours, whose? What the boss thinks is important to staff members. They want to feel their supervisor cares about them, understands what they do and knows when they have done it well. They want to feel appreciated for their contributions and achievements by the person whose opinion matters most.

Excuse #8: I don't want to make anyone feel uncomfortable by singling them out for recognition—Good point! While some people enjoy public recognition, others don't. Learn the recognition preferences of the people who work with you. Do they prefer to be recognized publicly or in private?

There are alternatives to public recognition: deliver it during a one-on-one meeting in your office, in a thank-you note, or in a message of appreciation written on a sticky note attached to their computer.

Excuse #9: I don't have any money in the budget for recognition—Simple, frequent recognition always trumps expensive but infrequent recognition. There are hundreds of ways to recognize staff which recipients will value, but which cost little or nothing at all. What's important is that recognition is inspired by a **Genuine** sense of appreciation and that it's strengthened by being **Relevant, Explicit, Appropriate and Timely**—in other words, it's **GREAT** staff recognition. For tips on providing more recognition on a limited budget, see Theme #25: A Penny-Pincher's Guide to Staff Recognition (p. 145).

Excuse #10: I don't feel comfortable recognizing staff—If recognition is new to you, it may not feel natural to thank people for a job well done. Try it. Practise on family and friends before taking your new skill into the workplace. Eventually, you will feel comfortable recognizing staff and become better at it. Even when done poorly, recognition motivated by a **Genuine** sense of appreciation is better than no recognition at all.

Excuse #11: I don't see anyone else recognizing staff—You know that more recognition is needed, but those around you aren't committed to recognizing staff. Don't wait for others to take the lead. Recognize excellent work when you see it. You don't need anyone else's permission to acknowledge work well done. In the words of Mahatma Gandhi, "Be the change you want to see in the world."

***

> **A Final Thought**
> Who do you know who appears hesitant to recognize staff? Schedule a meeting to discuss their reluctance to recognize. Ask why. Help them understand why their reasons for not recognizing staff are not as valid as they think they are.

Theme #28
Practices to Avoid When Recognizing Staff

No one wants to recognize staff in ways they won't value, which sometimes happens when leaders approach recognition in ways that diminish the impact of their intended message. Here are practices to avoid:

Father-knows-best attitude—Who better than you to decide how best to recognize staff? After all, you're the boss. You've experienced recognition on the way to your current position. You loved being congratulated in front of your peers. You appreciated receiving those golf balls bearing the company logo. Surely what worked for you will work for everyone.

Not so fast. You may love to hit the links every weekend, but look around. Not everyone golfs. For them, the reward will only come when someone buys those golf balls at their next garage sale.

And what about public recognition? Some people love it, while introverts will do anything to avoid it.

Basing recognition on your interests and recognition preferences could deny whole groups of individuals their opportunities for meaningful recognition. Get to know everyone's unique interests and their preference for public or private recognition. Recognition is most meaningful when it reflects what is important to the recipient, not to the person providing the recognition. For tips on how to get to know your staff, see Theme #9: Discovering the Most Appropriate Ways to Recognize Staff (p 53).

Trophies, certificates and banquets—Service awards and employee-of-the-month programs may be popular ways to recognize staff, but there is little evidence that recipients value them. "I feel so appreciated working here because every five years I get to go to a service banquet. If it were not for that, I would have left years ago," said no one, ever.

Get more impact from the time and money you devote to staff recognition by providing frequent informal recognition. Staff will value day-to-day expressions of gratitude more than infrequent formal recognition.

Making it about you—Standing before the staff, a boss bragged about how she recognized them, listing nearly every time she acknowledged the contributions of individuals and teams. Few in the audience appeared impressed. Recognition is never about you—it's about the people you are recognizing. It's okay to congratulate yourself for doing a swell job of recognizing staff, but do so in private. Anyone who has time to talk about what they are doing to recognize staff likely isn't spending enough time actually doing it.

A task to be crossed off a to-do list—The goal with to-do lists is to cross off tasks as completed. "Recognize staff" is the exception. This task should be on every daily to-do list, but it will never be crossed off because the need for recognition is always there. Staff members and teams will continue to contribute and achieve outcomes that merit thanks or congratulations. Recognition is never, "all done!"

Creating losers—One manager enthusiastically described how every staff member he recognized was automatically entered into a month-end draw for a big prize. "It's so exciting!" For the winner, yes, but not so much for those whose worthy contributions were not rewarded. We call those people "losers." Creating a bunch of losers is not a successful formula for building employee engagement.

Only recognizing some—It's a fact: some people do more. They should be recognized more often, but they should not be the only ones recognized. The contributions and achievements of others may be less significant or occur less frequently, but when they do occur, recognize them! If people never contribute in ways worthy of recognition, why are they still on your staff?

Recognition without knowing—Managers who believe that they can recognize everyone the same way at the same time might be shocked to learn about the cynicism stirred by such gestures. When everyone receives form letters thanking them for their "great work," their likely response is, "The boss doesn't know what I do and may not even know who I am." The larger the organization and the greater the distance in the hierarchy between the sender and the recipient, the greater the feeling of skepticism about the message.

There are, of course, times when team-wide celebrations of the successful completion of a project or for surviving a particularly challenging time are appropriate. Then the message must be clear—we are celebrating what the team achieved together.

When recognizing the contributions of individuals, the message should include a specific description of what the recipients did (i.e., be **Explicit**). Doing so demonstrates you are paying attention and know what each person does.

Only when wearing a "staff recognition hat"—You can't turn staff recognition on and off. Recognition must be ingrained in who you are—a habit of recognizing success whenever you see it. For the grouch who roams the workplace ignoring everyone and everything they do until 3:00 p.m. on Thursday, when staff recognition is scheduled, communicating messages of appreciation successfully will be a huge challenge. When the message is inconsistent with the behaviour staff see daily, it will be dismissed as insincere—not **Genuine**.

Believing that "one size fits all"—That's not true for clothing and it's not true for staff recognition. No two staff members are alike. Everyone has distinctive characteristics. Recognition that fits one may not be a good match to a colleague's recognition preference or reflect what's important to them. Recognition that is **Appropriate** is more memorable than when everyone receives the same generic award. One-size-fits-all recognition doesn't work.

Delegating recognition—If you are a senior executive, it's reasonable to expect that others who report to you will recognize those they supervise. But this doesn't absolve you of the responsibility for recognizing staff, particularly your direct reports. If you are not modelling recognition, who will believe it is important? Check out Theme #4: Senior Executives, Frontline Staff and

Recognition (p. 29) for more on the vital role of senior leaders in supporting and encouraging recognition throughout the organization.

Providing recognition that is undeserved—Saying, "You're doing a great job" to someone when it is untrue comes across as insincere. It damages your ability to provide **Genuine** recognition in the future—to this individual and to the rest of your team. Address underperformance the same way you praise superior performance. The feedback should be timely (don't save a heap of negative feedback to dump on an employee during their annual performance review). Make it specific. Describe what the employee did, why it fails to meet expectations, or how it was inconsistent with the organization's core values and why performance must improve.

Believing that recognition is a generational thing—Beware of generalizations such as, "Millennials need more recognition." Generalizations help you guess what people want, but staff recognition is not about which generation staff members belong to. You're dealing with individuals, each of whom has their own recognition needs and preferences. Whether they are baby boomers or millennials or belong to Generation X or Generation Z, they all want recognition for the work they do. They will work harder when they feel appreciated.

> **A Final Thought**
> Recognition should be proportional to what staff members achieved or how they contributed. Sometimes all that's needed is a pat on the back, a few words of acknowledgement, or a quick text. Other times, you may want to send a thank-you note, buy a coffee, or leave a treat on their desks. Sometimes a gift may be an **Appropriate** way to say thank you.

Theme #29
A Verbal Eraser and Other Words that are Barriers to Staff Recognition

> *"(Aunt Polly) said, 'Well, I never. There's no getting round it, you can work when you're a mind to, Tom.' Then she diluted the compliment by adding, 'But it's powerful seldom you're mind to, I'm bound to say.'"*
>
> — Mark Twain, *The Adventures of Tom Sawyer*

Attempts at recognizing staff can be derailed with a single three-letter word. Other phrases can dim the glow of intended messages of appreciation:

"But"—This word is the equivalent of a verbal eraser. Everything that went before this simple conjunction is forgotten as the focus shifts to what follows. "You did a great job on this report, *but it was late!*" What does the recipient hear? "You were late!" And how are the words that went before interpreted? As an insincere effort to soften the blow of criticism, that's how.

"You usually do a good job, however (INSERT CRITICISM HERE). General speaking, you're effective in your job"—Known as the "sandwich technique," this is based on ill-considered advice: "Always sandwich criticism between two layers of praise." Recipients soon catch on that the only purpose of the praise is to buffer bad news. It doesn't work. Sandwiches are all about what's in the middle. No one thinks first about the bread that holds the filling. Using the sandwich technique risks all future attempts at recognition being dismissed as insincere. Staff previously exposed to the sandwich technique will wait for the "second shoe to drop" whenever they hear your praise.

"You did a great job on this project! Now I need you to . . ."—When praise is immediately followed by a new assignment, recipients are cheated of the opportunity to savour the fine feeling that comes from being recognized. Recognition becomes a setup for more work and not appreciation for a job well done.

"I don't really know you, but I understand you do a good job"—These words generate so many questions in the recipient's mind. Who are you to be recognizing me? How do you know I do a good job? Who told you? Why do they think I do a good job? Why didn't they tell me themselves? Do you really believe what you are saying?

"Thanks for everything you do"—You might as well say, "Thank you for nothing in particular." Recipients might realize they're being (clumsily) thanked, but the message would be far stronger if it was **Explicit**, identifying one or two ways in which the recipient contributes.

"I don't really know what you do"—Recipients perceive recognition that begins this way as insincere. If you don't know what I do, how can you know that I do it well? Aren't you just going through the motions?

"There are so many people deserving of this award"—The intent of these words is to make people feel less disappointed they didn't receive the award, but instead they are wondering, "How was this person chosen for this award? Why not me?" And the recipient thinks, "If others were just as deserving, my contribution wasn't as special as I thought."

"Deciding who should receive this award was difficult"—This may be true, but who cares? Making tough decisions is what leadership is about. It would mean more to recipients to hear that the decision was easy because of the quality of their contribution or achievement.

***

A Final Thought
Ensure your message of appreciation has the desired impact by avoiding words and phrases that deflate expressions of appreciation. Say nothing that will make your message feel less sincere.

Theme #30
Avoiding the "Participation Ribbon" Trap

> *"Those of us who were too weak, too heavy or too uncoordinated to warrant a bronze (medal in the Canada Fitness Award Program) received a little plastic pin with the letter P on it. P for participant. Cue the public shaming."*
>
> — Rick Mercer, *Talking to Canadians*

Treating all staff members fairly doesn't mean everyone should be treated the same. Don't become one of those managers who feel that all staff should receive recognition in the same way and at the same time. They believe that by treating all employees equally they will avoid upsetting staff who are not being recognized. They don't want anyone to be upset because they didn't receive the same recognition as their colleagues.

The fact is, not all contributions and achievements are equally significant to the organization's success. Leaders should be more worried about how top performers feel when they see those who contributed less receiving identical recognition.

Unlike paycheques, benefits or having a physically and emotionally safe work environment, recognition is not an entitlement. It must be "earned" by staff contributing in ways that leaders and co-workers appreciate. Recognize staff for actions that you want to see repeated.

Recognition should also be proportionate to what the recipient did. This means certain staff members will be recognized more frequently and in more significant ways than others.

Doing otherwise would turn recognition into a participation ribbon exercise—providing recognition for everyone who showed up. While this is common in children's sports, it's a practice to avoid if recognition is to be **Genuine:**

Accept that staff members contribute in different ways and they deserve to be recognized differently.

***

> **Why You Shouldn't Recognize Everyone the Same Way**
>
> Recognizing everyone the same way ignores two realities of any workplace:
> - People perform differently. Different people produce different results. Each person has unique strengths, meaning they perform some tasks better than others.
> - People have different recognition preferences: private versus public; a letter placed in one's personnel file versus a handwritten thank-you card; a pat on the back versus a coffee card.
>
> Recognition should reflect the significance and quality of the individual's contribution and their recognition preferences. To recognize all staff in the same way shortchanges your top performers, inflates the value of what underperformers do and ignores the fact that the team is made up of individuals—each with their own recognition preferences.

Avoid an "everyone-gets-a-turn" approach to recognition. Recognize staff only when it's deserved.

***

Recognize staff members whenever what they did contributes to the organization's success or demonstrates behaviours that reflect the organization's values.

***

Be alert for less obvious but still important contributions by "quieter" staff members to ensure these are not overlooked.

***

Be specific when describing what recipients did. **Explicit** recognition makes it clear why particular staff members deserve recognition now, while others do not.

Keep track of who you recognize, how and why. Who are you missing? Why are they not being recognized? Are you the problem, or are they? If you can't find a reason to recognize a staff member, consider this as evidence that there may be a performance problem that needs addressing.

***

Don't force it. Don't recognize someone who has done nothing deserving of recognition. Limit the time at staff meetings scheduled for peer recognition, cutting it off before the staff runs out of reasons to recognize colleagues. Don't force staff to invent reasons to recognize their colleagues.

***

> **A Final Thought**
> Being fair doesn't mean treating everyone the same—just fairly. Don't keep a score card to ensure everyone receives the same amount of recognition. Accept that people contribute in different ways and to different levels, so some may deserve more recognition than others. If the recognition is deserved, you're not playing favourites.

Bonus Section
At Least 101 More Staff Recognition Thoughts, Tips, Tools and Techniques

Phrases such as, "our first priority is serving customers," or "the customer comes first," are common in the world of retail. They may sound good, but for supervisors, the focus should be closer to home. If you want staff to make serving customers their priority—and it should be if you want customers to keep doing business with you—make your staff a priority. People who feel they are well-treated, valued and appreciated are more likely to treat customers well. When you treat customers well, they remain loyal. Treat staff well and they will stay. Customer loyalty and staff retention are both keys to an organization's success.

***

When your work group faces a tough task that will require longer hours or extra effort, find techniques to recognize members along the way for their commitment. Deliver treats to their workstations. Be present to encourage and praise their efforts. Provide lunch when they must work extra hours or over the weekend. Celebrate the successful conclusion to the project.

***

Create a staff recognition team, responsible for finding new ways to recognize staff. Remind them of the five ingredients that make recognition **GREAT**—Genuine, Relevant, Explicit, Appropriate and Timely. Provide them with a small budget and your support. Become a champion for their ideas.

Remember that what they do should supplement, not replace, the recognition you provide.

***

Celebrate achieving 100. It could be with 100 candies, 100 flowers, or 100 dollars for having reached 100 per cent of a goal or a project, or for having completed one hundred days in a new job.

***

Provide opportunities for staff to learn from each other. Did someone develop a new way to complete a routine task, an idea to save time or money, or a better approach to serving customers? Invite them to present their idea to the rest of the team.

***

Rather than simply leaving paycheques or pay advisories in employees' mailboxes, hand deliver them personally, along with a few words of thanks. Another time, attach a handwritten thank-you note to the paycheque.

***

Leave notes of appreciation on staff members' desks.

***

Recognition is more memorable when it is customized for the event, for the achievement and for the recipient.

***

Demonstrate your appreciation by picking up a drink from a staff member's favourite coffee shop. Write a short message of appreciation on the cup.

***

Recognize behaviours you want to see more often. Staff members who feel appreciated are more likely to perform in ways you want them to perform.

***

When you know where staff members will be staying while on a business trip, arrange for a small token of appreciation to be waiting when they arrive, such as a thank-you note or treat to enjoy after they check in.

***

Part of what makes recognition special is that it's spontaneous. Recipients don't see it coming. It can occur anytime and anywhere—whenever they have done something that deserves to be acknowledged.

***

Things don't always go as we wish. At these times, it's important to remain positive. There are always reasons to recognize others.

***

Have co-workers sign a company T-shirt and present it to a staff member to mark an employment milestone or completion of a project.

***

When recognition depends on nominations from peers and customers, being nominated is often more important than the resulting award. Ensure that nominees know about all the nominations that they receive. Share the nominations with the nominees.

***

Don't wait until that big project is complete to celebrate the team's success. Keep the team energized and focused on the goal by celebrating progress. Big projects consist of small tasks that need to be accomplished well so that the larger goal can be achieved. Take time along the way to acknowledge those small successes. Doing so confirms to everyone that they are on the right track and energizes them to continue the journey.

***

If you can't remember the last time that you recognized an individual, it's likely been too long. Time to search for a reason to praise this person for what they achieved or how they contributed.

***

Be ever-vigilant—constantly on the lookout for what staff members are doing well. When you look for them, you will find reasons to recognize staff.

***

Add a letter noting a contribution to a staff member's permanent file, remembering to send a copy to that person.

***

Before heading home, list what went well during the day. Who was responsible? How will you recognize those people tomorrow?

***

Pause at the end of the week (or month) to reflect on recent successes. Who was responsible? How did you express your appreciation for their contribution? Didn't recognize them? No problem. Do it now!

***

Searching for inspiration on how to recognize a staff member? Consider going back to the future. How have you recognized others in the past (or how have you been recognized?) Would one of those techniques be **Appropriate** for this individual?

***

Tell your boss (or your boss's boss) about a specific contribution or achievement by an individual staff member. Request that they drop by the deserving staff member's desk to congratulate them on a job well done and suggest that they keep this capable staff member in mind when there is an opportunity for a promotion.

***

An email or phone call from a senior manager isn't as good as a personal visit, but it is still an effective way to say, "Well done!" Ask your boss (or your boss's boss) to send those emails or make those calls.

***

What attribute does each person bring to the team that makes it successful? At a team meeting, acknowledge one attribute of each team member that you appreciate.

***

Effective brainstorming sessions or staff meeting discussions depend on the willingness of people to participate and make suggestions. So let those who offered input know that their involvement and ideas were appreciated. "Thank you for your idea about [topic being discussed] during our staff meeting. It really helped explain what we are doing."

***

What would bump your department up from good to great? Brainstorm answers with staff to identify the steps to get there. Thank them for their input and then recognize behaviours that align with the strategies staff identified.

***

When a staff member is facing a tight timeline which will require putting in extra hours, offer to stay late to help, or take on routine tasks to provide the other person more time during the workday to tackle the project.

***

When you recognize staff for generating clever ideas, they will come up with more good ideas. Research by American firm O.C. Tanner, which develops strategic employee recognition for clients worldwide, found that employees who receive "strong recognition" will "generate two times as many ideas per month compared to those who aren't recognized as well."

***

Support staff members who have chosen to change a bad habit (for example, quitting smoking) by recognizing them whenever you see progress toward the new behaviour.

***

Celebrate success with a balloon bouquet.

***

Start with a staff list. For each person, identify one contribution they have made recently that you appreciate. Then recognize them for what they did.

***

Expressing appreciation to staff and co-workers is important, but don't forget other people in your life. Practise recognition everywhere and with everyone. Express appreciation to friends, family members and others you encounter in your daily life. They will feel good hearing your words and you will be sharpening the skills you use to recognize the contributions and achievements of staff and colleagues.

***

See your workplace from different perspectives. Change your routine. Enter via a different door. Take a different route to your desk or office. Stop to speak with people whose workstations you don't normally pass. What are they doing? Do you see anything for which they could be recognized? Change the time at which you take your break. Sit next to someone different than your normal companions. What can you learn about this person you didn't already know? By changing your behaviour, you will discover ways in which staff contribute of which you were unaware. Then you'll have new reasons to recognize staff.

***

It can hit you anytime—in the evening, during the weekend, or when you are away from the workplace. You realize that a staff member performed well, but you didn't say anything at the time. To avoid forgetting to recognize this person at the next opportunity, jot down a brief note or send yourself a reminder email. Or record a short video message on your phone now, that you can schedule to be emailed or texted at the beginning of the next work day.

***

Create an album or a scrapbook of photos and other items that tell the story of a staff member's successes. Present the book when the person reaches a significant employment milestone, retires, or leaves because of a family move to another community.

***

Say thank you by offering a deserving employee a prime parking space for a day, a week or a month.

***

Recognize staff members' expertise by providing them with an opportunity to use this expertise to make a decision.

***

Arrange for a caricature artist to draw portraits of team members to celebrate their success or employment milestones. Encourage the artist to include items that reflect the individual's interests and hobbies. It's a gift they won't soon discard.

***

Staff will look forward to Monday mornings if you consistently arrive early to leave notes on their desks, expressing appreciation for what they did the previous week.

***

Surprise staff members with recognition texts on the weekend. "Just couldn't wait until Monday to let you how impressed I was with the description you wrote of our new product. Easy to understand how people will benefit from using it. Well done!"

***

Take recognition out of the office. Meet for coffee in a nearby park. Go for lunch. Just take a walk. While you are away from the usual work setting, describe a contribution the person made that you appreciate.

***

Say thank you to staff members with a gesture that will last for 12 months: a subscription to their favourite magazine. When the magazine arrives each month, they will be reminded of your appreciation for what they did.

***

Improve the ratio between the positive and negative feedback you provide. Strive to praise two, three, or more times more often than you criticize an individual's performance. A study by Emily Heaphy and Marcial Losada from Harvard University found that praise/criticism on high performing teams was 5.6/1, compared to a 0.36/1 ratio on teams they described as low performing. Achieving a higher ratio of praise to criticism should boost morale and help establish a positive workplace culture.

***

Staff members who know that their work is being monitored so that effective work can be celebrated are more likely to become more engaged in their work.

***

When you are open to the opportunities that present themselves, you can learn a great deal from your staff. They may have discovered easier or more efficient ways to complete tasks. Observe what they do. Ask questions. Use what you learn. Follow up with a thank-you note to your "teacher." When you share your new knowledge with others, credit the person from whom you learned.

***

Who have you not recognized recently? Why not? If they haven't done anything recognition-worthy, that's one thing (which may need to be addressed). On the other hand, if it is simply because you have been overlooking the person's contributions, make a commitment to recognize this individual at least once in the next 48 hours.

***

A hockey ritual is to name three stars at the end of each game, based on how well they played. There is always an explanation of what they did well ("scored two goals and assisted on another," or "stopped 42 shots on the way to a shutout.") Consider selecting your own three stars, based on how well they did their jobs that day or week. How did they contribute? What did they achieve?

***

You may have seen name tags that inform customers that the person serving them is new or a "trainee." It lets us know we are dealing with someone who is still learning and who needs us to be patient. On the other hand, we seldom see anything that identifies longer-term staff members. Provide name badges to let customers know that their server or customer service agent is someone who has been a loyal employee for five years, or to inform parents that their children are being taught by a teacher who has earned a master's degree in education. Update badges when staff members reach new service anniversaries, complete other training or receive awards.

***

Keep your camera handy to capture pictures of team members hard at work. Text the photo, along with your words of appreciation, to the staff members.

Post the photos in a location that staff members frequent. Put together a staff memory book.

***

Be alert for staff members who are feeling frustrated with their work. The source of their frustration may be just one aspect of their job that's not going well. Meet with them over coffee or lunch to discuss how they feel, but also use this an opportunity to remind them of recent successes. Restate your appreciation for how they have contributed and that they are valued members of the staff. Help them put everything into perspective.

***

You have probably heard the advice, "Don't sweat the small things." Keep this in mind the next time a staff member leaves two or three loose ends. Rather than dwelling on these small omissions, focus on what they achieved. Praise the success. Don't make a big deal out of the trivial things.

***

Include stories about team members' contributions and successes on your website. Update frequently.

***

Reserve space in your internal newsletter to acknowledge the contributions and achievements of your staff, both at work and out in the community.

***

Pick up the telephone and call staff members just to tell them how much their work is appreciated.

***

You can always buy a treat for the staff on the way to work, which is a pleasant thing to do, but it's more special when you arrive with cookies you baked yourself.

***

Demonstrate your trust and respect for staff by stepping back and allowing them to take ownership of their assignments. But don't back off too far. You want to be there to congratulate them on a job well done.

Greet retirees and former employees who drop by for a visit. Make a bit of a fuss over them. Introduce them to recent hires. You will be reminding the visitors they were valued staff members and will show current staff that appreciation doesn't end the day people step out the door.

***

Go a step beyond just posting photos of staff members with names and job titles in your reception area. Include descriptions of their recent achievements and contributions.

***

What is it about their jobs that staff members are most enthusiastic about? Find out by asking them. In many cases, it will be something they do well—something for which you can recognize them. The best way to recognize them may be to find more opportunities for them to do the type of work they enjoy.

***

Be alert for staff members who are feeling frustrated with their work. The source of their frustration may be just one aspect of their job that's not going well. Meet with them to discuss what they are feeling. Use this opportunity to remind them of recent successes and restate your appreciation for how they have contributed and why they are valued members of the staff. Help them put everything into perspective.

***

Feeling stressed? Taking a moment to recognize someone for a job well done is a great stress reliever.

***

One of the questions The Gallup Organization asks to measure employee engagement is, "In the last seven days, have you received recognition or praise for good work?" How would your staff answer?

***

Occasionally, when you send an email to staff members, add a postscript (P.S.) in which you express appreciation for something they did and why it was important.

***

Is an approaching deadline creating stress for members of your team? It may be a suitable time to remind them what has gone well, so far and to express your confidence in their ability to bring the project to a successful conclusion.

***

Some tasks are not particularly enjoyable or desirable but they must still be done. Occasionally, express your gratitude with an offer to take on one of these tasks for a staff member.

***

Jot down what staff members do well, individually and as a team. Refer to your list prior to meeting with individuals or the team. Reasons to recognize will be fresh in your mind.

***

Think about your staff. What unique contributions does each staff member make? What does each do well? Hopefully, everyone does at least one aspect of the job well. (If not, you should question why you keep this employee around, but that's a topic for another day.) Write a brief description of how each person contributes. Create a display of staff photos, with captions that describe how the individual pictured contributed.

***

Five decades later, I still recall what happened at the end of the final day of my first year as a teacher. The students were gone and we had spent the day in meetings, tidying our classrooms and preparing to begin the new school year in a few weeks' time. Standing at the front door as we made our way to the parking lot to begin our summer vacation was the principal. He shook everyone's hand and thanked us for our contributions over the past ten months. I left feeling valued and appreciated and looking forward to returning to *his school* in the fall.

***

It's Friday, the end of a week when things have gone well. Sales may be up, a customer survey has revealed a high level of satisfaction, or a special event came off without a hitch. Before this day ends and everyone heads home for the weekend, take time to say thank you to the team for how it contributed to making the week a success. Make an announcement. Leave a voice mail or send everyone an email. Hold a short staff meeting to express your gratitude for what went well. No matter how you celebrate a week's worth of success, you will be ending the week on a positive note. Whatever happens last is what staff will remember best about their week at work.

***

Before you leave at the end of the day, or before the staff arrives in the morning, display a poster-sized thank-you note in the staff room or at a staff member's desk, where it will be the first thing the person and co-workers see when they get to work.

***

What aspect of their work makes your staff most enthusiastic? Find out. Often what people enjoy most are those tasks which they do best, which suggests where to look for efforts and results deserving of recognition.

***

Who fills in for staff members who are temporarily absent due to vacations, illness or other reasons? These individuals—substitute teachers, nurses who work occasional shifts, or on-call workers who fill in for a few days—are important to keep everything running smoothly until the permanent staff returns. Let them know that you appreciate their availability and what they do while they are there.

Greet them when they arrive and show them to their workstation for the day. Tell them who to approach if they have questions. Check in to see how the day is going. Spend a moment at the end of the shift to thank them for their assistance.

***

"We shall never know all the good that a simple smile can do."

- Saint Teresa of Calcutta

A friendly greeting in the morning can get a person's day off to a good start. Don't underestimate the impact that a smile and a handful of kind words have on whether a staff member feels valued or not.

***

Everyone should be recognized from time to time, but finding a reason to recognize certain individuals can be a challenge. Their work is acceptable, but nothing jumps out as being truly recognition worthy. It's time to prime the pump. Assign a task that you are confident they will do well. Monitor their progress and encourage them, as necessary. When they complete the task successfully, be ready with **Timely** recognition. Who knows? Your recognition just might be the catalyst that lifts their performance to another level. Next time, it will be easier to find a reason to recognize them.

***

Make expressing gratitude to your staff a key topic on all your social media channels.

***

Occasionally, when recognizing a staff member in writing for a job well done, place a copy of your letter or note in the person's personnel file where a future supervisor may read it.

***

A promotion is sometimes the recognition staff members receive for consistently performing at a level that meets or exceeds expectations. But what if there are no vacant positions for top performers who are seeking a new challenge? Rather than lose them to another organization, what about a lateral move to another department? It will be an opportunity for valued staff members to learn new skills that will make them more successful when an opportunity for promotion does present itself.

***

On her grandmother's 100th birthday, a granddaughter presented her with a scrapbook that included photographs that captured the ten decades of her life. It's an idea that could be adapted in many workplaces—a memory book presented to an employee who reaches a significant service anniversary (five, ten, fifteen or twenty years), or who is retiring after a lengthy career. Include photographs, comments from co-workers and customers and a timeline that shows key events and achievements that occurred during this employee's tenure.

***

The coach of a youth hockey team wrapped up the year with awards for all the players, each of which reflected the player's unique contribution to the team. There were the usual awards that you would expect, such as "Most goals" and "Most assists." Other awards showed that the coach noticed what the player did: "Top face-off man," "Best at congratulating teammates for a good game," or "Most defensive forward." Could you do something similar for your work team? "Most willing to help a colleague," or "Most able to 'stay calm and carry on' in stressful situations," or "Best at organizing social events?"

***

Are you taking full advantage of the skills of team members? Is there some way to reorganize workloads so that all employees get some tasks they enjoy and do well?

***

Heard any great ideas recently? Are you able to implement one of them? Ensure that the person who made the suggestion gets credit. If possible, involve this person in planning and implementing the innovation.

***

What are the metrics that you use to assess your organization's success? As you collect this information, share it with the team. Describe how what they do is **Relevant** to the organization's success.

***

Flowers—in a bouquet or as a single bloom—are always a wonderful way to acknowledge contributions.

***

At the end of the day, ask staff members what went well that day. Congratulate them on their success. You might also ask: "What was one thing that you learned today?" "What did you notice today that we could do differently that would make your job easier or improve the customer's experience?" Asking these questions demonstrates your respect for staff members and that you value their opinions. And as a bonus, you may discover an idea for an innovation that has a significant impact on your organization's success.

***

Create a "business card" with a simple message, such as, "Great job!" or "You did something impressive today." Personalize the message with a short, handwritten description of what the person did. It's a quick way to make a person's day.

***

A school vice-principal uses acronyms to show appreciation to her staff. She begins by selecting an inspirational word that is appropriate for an individual. Next, she carefully chooses other words that begin with the letters of the acronym that described the person she wishes to honour. It takes a bit of time, but the messages of appreciation are well-received by the recipients.

***

Does the geography of the workplace influence the amount of recognition individuals receive? Do people who work closer to the boss's desk receive more recognition than those who are further away? To reduce the impact of proximity, leave your office regularly to visit staff members whose workspaces are furthest from your office. Find out what they do for which they deserve to be recognized.

***

Invite someone who does a task well to mentor colleagues, but only if teaching others is something the employee enjoys. Forcing someone who is uncomfortable with this role to mentor others is the equivalent of punishing someone for being successful.

***

When hockey players perform well and work hard, coaches give them what they want most: more ice time; maybe time on the power play. How can you acknowledge your team members who perform well with more of the type of work they enjoy most?

***

Just because it's after hours when you discover Sarah has done an excellent job on that important task you assigned her, it's no excuse to put off expressing appreciation until tomorrow. Pick up the phone and call her at home. She's not home? Leave her a message. Tell her how much you appreciate what she did.

Not comfortable calling staff at home? Leave a message on her work voice mail so your expression of appreciation greets her first thing in the morning. This would certainly be a positive start to her day.

***

Follow up annual performance reviews with handwritten notes highlighting some of the staff members' successes of the past year.

***

The manager of a local coffee shop used the video screen on which it advertised new drinks and specials to celebrate the achievement of two staff members. He included photos of two, "newly certified baristas" in the rotation of images. Adapt this idea for your workplace:
- Acknowledge staff that has recently completed specialized training
- Congratulate those who have received a college diploma or earned a university degree
- Recognize a team that brought a project to a successful conclusion
- Celebrate employees who have reached a service milestone or are about to retire
- Welcome new people to your team

No screen on which to display your information? No problem. Go old school and use a bulletin board to display this information.

***

Create a lapel pin with a design that captures the essence of your organization's core values. Award the pin to individuals whose behaviour consistently reflects these values. Some suggested designs for the pin:
- A target graphic for a company that is committed to providing customer service that is, "on the mark"

- A hot-air balloon for an organization that offers products or services that, "rise above the crowd"
- Crossed hockey sticks, a basketball or other sports-inspired images for an organization that emphasizes teamwork

***

Be clear about why you are recognizing staff. Unless you are specific about what the recipients did (**Explicit**) and why it is important (**Relevant**), your gesture of appreciation is merely, "a nice thing to do." There is nothing wrong with doing something "nice," but you will have missed the opportunity to demonstrate that you are aware of how staff contributes and the opportunity to remind staff that what they do is relevant to the organization's success.

***

Allow staff to decide how best to use time that is designated for professional development.

***

> *"Write a note on a whiteboard in the staff room or in the classroom where students will see it."*
>
> – Anonymous program participant

***

When a staff member does something extra to meet a customer's needs (additional research, comes in early or on the weekend, or takes steps to ensure on-time delivery), thank her in front of the customer, if possible. Describe how the service provider went beyond the call of duty for the customer. "Jake, you may not know this, but Kaley skipped lunch yesterday to drive across town to pick up the widgets you required from our supplier. She knew that you really needed them and wanted to be sure you received them right away. We really appreciate that Kaley was willing to go the extra mile—figuratively and literally—to meet our customer's needs."

***

Things don't always go as we might wish. At these times, it's important to remain positive. There are always reasons to recognize others.

***

Discovering you haven't been finding time to recognize staff recently? It may be time to renew your commitment by setting new recognition goals.

***

Learn about what's happening in staff members' lives. The more you know, the better you can be there when they need you.

***

> **Recognize Each Person's Uniqueness**
>
> What special non-work talents do staff members have? Demonstrate that you value each individual's uniqueness by providing opportunities for them to showcase what makes them unique:
> - Invite the staff member with a green thumb to share gardening tips
> - Arrange an art show for your resident artist, or commission a painting for your reception area
> - Schedule a musically talented staff member to perform a lunch-hour concert
> - Provide ingredients so staff members can demonstrate their skills as a chef by preparing a special staff lunch
> - Ask a staff member who is known for the quality of their photography to explain how to take better vacation photos

Think of Mondays, or the first or the month, as times to revisit and refresh your goals (including those related to staff recognition).

***

Offer financial or material support so that staff members can enhance their work area. These enhancements may make the recipient's work area more comfortable, the work easier and the staff member happier and more productive.

***

Solicit top performers' input when you have a position to fill. What competencies should the new person possess? Invite them to join the interview panel and involve them in deciding the right person to hire.

***

Involve staff in writing procedure manuals. Be sure to credit them as contributors to the resulting document.

***

Send top performers to visit another department, school or clinic with the object of finding better ways to complete tasks. Ask them what they learned and how it might apply to your organization.

***

Business cards should not be limited to a select few who have achieved certain "status" within the organization. Provide business cards for everyone to show that they are important members of the team.

***

Say thank you for a tough job done well by offering a staff member the opportunity to take on an easier task. Sometimes we punish success with another tough assignment.

***

What are staff members' areas of expertise? Designate them as "our expert in _____." Let others know that this is the person to go to if they have questions.

***

Why do we wait until someone is dead to honour them with plaques on park benches dedicated to their memory, or by planting a tree in their name? There's no rule that says we can't name something such as a bench, meeting room or a piece of equipment in honour of someone who has and continues to contribute to the organization's success.

***

Take a storyteller's approach to praise. Tell tales of success that begin with a description of the challenge a staff member faced ("Once upon a time, there was a customer with a need that was difficult to meet . . .") Continue with an explanation of how the challenge was overcome and how this resulted in "everyone living happily ever after."

***

Staff members know when certain employees are not pulling their weight or are poisoning the work environment and they expect their supervisors to act. When they perceive that you tolerate underperformance and negative behaviour, those who do work hard to meet expectations may feel discouraged. Address performance problems when you become aware of them.

***

Conventional wisdom says we are shouting when we type words in UPPERCASE. So what's wrong with occasionally shouting about appreciating a JOB WELL DONE in text messages, emails and even in written thank-you notes? <u>Underlining,</u> **bold type and** exclamation marks work too, as long as you **<u>DON'T OVERDO IT!!!!!</u>**

***

Ask staff for their input and opinions. "You are always successful at what you do and certainly understand your job better than I do, so I would welcome any suggestions you have to improve how work is done or how we could make the work easier for you and others."

***

Acknowledge staff members' contributions by asking them to represent you or the organization by hosting a visitor, such as a parent new to the school or an important customer. They can give the visitor a tour, answer questions and take them to lunch.

***

If you're not sure what people have done for which they deserve to be recognized, ask them. "I know you work hard and I believe that there must be a recent contribution or achievement that stands out in your mind as worthy of recognition, which I may have missed. Tell me about it." Thank them for sharing the information and for what was accomplished.

***

Pitch stories about your staff members' accomplishments to the local media. Reporters won't always follow up on your suggestions, but occasionally your tip may lead to a story that portrays both the individual and the organization in a positive light.

***

Put staff members forward to the local media as experts on particular topics. Reporters often look for a local angle to a national or international story and your staff members may be exactly the local expert they are looking for.

***

Let staff know how you feel about them, using powerful words such as "trust" and "pride."

***

When introducing staff members to visitors, senior managers or new staff, include examples of what they have accomplished or how they contribute.

***

Program your smartphone to send you a reminder to "Recognize someone today."

***

Time at staff meetings is commonly scheduled for staff members to acknowledge the contributions of their peers. That's great, but there should also be time when those in managerial positions express appreciation for how the team and individuals have contributed and what they have accomplished. When you are specific about these achievements and contributions, it shows you are really paying attention, which itself is a type of recognition. You will also be reminding other staff what is **Relevant** to the organization's success.

***

Staff members don't simply slip into an abyss at the end of the day, only to miraculously reappear to begin their next shift. They are individuals. They have lives away from the workplace, with outside interests and families. Acknowledge their non-work successes, such as finishing a marathon, appearing in an amateur theatre production (or helping behind the scenes), or having paintings included in a local art show. Congratulate them on non-work milestones (wedding anniversaries, children's graduations, etc.), celebrate the birth of a child or grandchild. You will be showing that you see them as individuals with lives outside work, not just cogs in the corporate machine.

***

For recognition that will remind recipients of your appreciation for an entire year, give them an annual pass to a museum or art gallery.

***

People are more engaged when you ask for their ideas and implement their suggestions.

***

Encourage innovative thinking and highlight those who come up with new ways of doing things by encouraging them to submit proposals to speak at an industry conference.

***

Install a whiteboard where staff pass by regularly. Write notes of appreciation and encourage others to do the same.

***

People remember best what occurred last. What happens last creates the greatest impression. End each day on a positive note. Leave a message of appreciation at a location staff will pass at the end of the day—by the time clock where they check out, at the exit to the parking lot, near the coat rack.

***

Think of your team as a jigsaw puzzle. Find where people fit best, based on their strengths. Change assignments if needed. A minor change can create a major positive change in attitude and work quality.

***

Show trust when you delegate to staff members. Provide clear expectations about the results and why those results are important to organizational success. Leave the how up to them. Then stay out of their way but let them know you're available for advice and assistance if required. And congratulate them on a job well done when they finish.

***

Some say that the use of the phrase "thank you" is rare. Is that true? Find out with this little experiment. Spend a day listening to how often you hear the words, "Thank you" (or "Thanks") wherever you are—at work, while shopping, at home or out in the community. How often do you hear something else, such as, "Have a good day," or "Here you go," or nothing at all?

***

Here's a variation on the previous experiment. For a day, keep track of the number of times you say, "Thank you." How many opportunities to say thank you did you miss?

***

Buy dinner for staff who are working late. Arrange for delivery to their homes. You're saying thank you in two ways—buying them dinner and saving them the time they would have spent preparing a meal.

***

Everyone busy? Feeling stressed? There may be no better time to recognize staff for their efforts and reaffirm that you value them for who they are and what they do.

***

Do other teams contribute to your team's success? How does your team express appreciation to the other team? Ask staff members to identify reasons to recognize other teams and suggest ways to provide interdepartmental recognition. Teams recognizing other teams help maintain and build interdepartmental relationships, improve communication and co-operation, and reduce interdepartmental conflict. Suggestions: leave an early morning snack for the other team or send a giant thank-you card that everyone has signed.

***

Recruitment ads that boast about current employees are good for morale and create the impression your workplace is a place where people want to be. Use current staff in company publications, annual reports, brochures, advertising, etc.

***

Demonstrate your respect for the opinions of current staff by seeking their input when preparing recruitment advertising and developing questions to ask during interviews.

***

Link staff recognition to your recruitment advertising. For example, one company included this message in its advertising: "The company with the best people wins . . . and that's us. We want you!"

***

Allow staff members with the best attendance record the first choice of shifts.

***

Post the names of members of the custodial staff who are responsible for keeping a specific area clean. "This hallway is sparkling clean because Trevor does such a fantastic job."

***

List all your staff members on your weekly to-do list with the intent of placing a checkmark next to each name during the week when you thank them for doing something you feel deserves recognition.

***

Tell staff members when ideas they suggested result in savings or increased profit. Calculate the impact of the suggestion to the bottom line.

***

Do staff members have unique skills from which other departments would benefit? Offer to "loan" them to another department, but only after getting the staff member's consent.

***

Within 24 hours of management meetings, share the discussion and decisions with staff. Answer their questions or commit to finding answers if you don't know. Sharing information makes everyone feel they are part of a team.

***

At the end of the day, ask staff members what went well. Remind them to congratulate themselves on a job well done.

***

Purchase tickets to allow staff members to take their families to a local museum or schedule an outing for the whole team.

***

> **A Final Thought**
> **Self-recognition.** Don't forget that even you, the boss, deserves recognition for the fine job you do. Keep track of what you accomplish each week. Quite an impressive list, isn't it? Take time to recognize yourself for how you contribute and what you achieve. Do something special just for yourself. You deserve it! Enjoy your favourite treat (and don't feel guilty about all those extra calories—you earned them!). Come in late or leave early. Go to a movie. Buy something special. Pick up that book you have been planning to read.

A Final Request
Become a Staff Recognition Evangelist!

Is recognition making a difference in your workplace? Is recognition contributing to building and maintaining a positive culture? Has more recognition made the team more productive? Is morale and engagement up? Is turnover down? Share your staff recognition success with other leaders. Encourage them to do more to recognize staff for how they contribute and what they achieve. Proclaim the good news. Spread the staff recognition message.

Notes

First, A Bit About You, the Reader

Page xi: "Research by Gallup and Workhuman found four of every five leaders . . ." Cari Nazeer (August 8, 2022) "The Recognition We All Want at Work," https://time.com/charter/6204417/employee-recognition/

Theme #1: Recognition Builds Workplace Relationships

Page 4: "The best teams care for and support . . ." Mark Messier and Jimmy Roberts, *No One Win Alone: A Memoir* (Toronto, Simon and Schuster, *2021*) p. 296.

Page 4: "Is your organization a good place to work?" Burchell, Michael and Robin, Jennifer, *The Great Workplace: How to build it, how to keep it and why it matters*, (San Francisco: Jossey-Bass, A Wiley Imprint, 2011) p. 21.

Page 4: "Research shows that 90 per cent of staff members who receive recognition . . ." William Craig (July 17, 2017) "3 Reasons Why Employee Recognition Will Always Matter."

Page 4: "42 per cent of Millennials . . ." Tracy Benson (February 11, 2016) "Motivating Millennials Takes More than Flexible Work Policies" https://hbr.org/2016/02/motivating-millennials-takes-more-than-flexible-work-policies

What is "Staff Recognition?"

Page 6: "Employee recognition is a key element of a successful business strategy . . ." https://www.recognition.org/RPI/RPI/About/About_Employee_Recognition.aspx

Page 6: "Recognition is defined as seeing . . ." Cindy Ventrice, *Make Their Day! Employee Recognition that Works (San Francisco: Berrett-Koehler, 2003).*

Page 6: "To acknowledge and appreciate those behaviors . . ." – Sue Glasscock and Kimberly Gram *Workplace Recognition: Step-by-step examples of a positive reinforcement strategy* (London: B.T. Batsford Ltd., 1999).

Page 7: "Recognition comes from the heart . . ." David Rye, *Attracting and Rewarding Outstanding Employees* (Santa Monica: Entrepreneur Press, 2002).

Page 7: "Recognition is a positive consequence . . ." Bob Nelson, *Recognizing & Engaging Employees for Dummies* (Hoboken: John Wiley and Sons, Ltd., 2015) p. 9.

Page 7: "Recognition is about noticing . . ." Achievers, downloaded from a webinar on October 27, 2022.

Theme #5: Making Staff Recognition a Habit

Page 33: "*Atomic Habits* author James Clear defines as 'a behaviour . . .'" James Clear, *Atomic Habits: An Easy & Proven Way to Build Good Habits & Break Bad Ones* (Avery, 2018), p. 44.

Page 33: "Productivity expert Hugh Culver compares developing a habit to lighting a fire…" Hugh Culver, Hero Habits (download for free at https://hughculver.com/do-you-have-hero-habits-10-questions-you-must-ask-yourself-today/

Theme #10: Linking Staff Recognition to Career Goals

Page 61: "The Gallup Organization found that one of the 12 predictors of successful organizations . . ." Rodd Wagner and James K. Harter, *12: The Elements of Great Managing* (New York: Gallup Press, 2006) p. 77.

Theme #15: A Year's Worth of Staff Recognition

Page 84: "I'm a big advocate of using recognition on a daily basis . . ." "How to Celebrate Employee Appreciation Day," https://www.triadadvertising.com/how-to-celebrate-employee-appreciation-day/

Theme #18: Staff Recognition Goes Green

Page 103: "British and Dutch researchers found that having office plants . . ." "Here's why you should take your houseplant to work," https://

www.news24.com/health24/lifestyle/healthy-workplace/at-the-office/heres-why-you-should-take-your-houseplant-to-work-20180118

Theme #19: Assessing Your Staff Recognition Practices

Page 126: "Research by OC Tanner suggests that many organizations are . . ." https://www.octanner.com/global-culture-report/2021/recognition.html

Theme #22: Diverse and Inclusive: Recognition for Workplaces Where Everyone Feels They Belong

Page 126: "Companies can mandate diversity, but they have to cultivate inclusion." Janet Stovall, TED Talk: How to get serious about diversity and inclusion in the workplace. https://www.youtube.com/watch?v=kvdHqS3ryw0

Page 126: "Michael Bach uses the words of American diversity and inclusion consultant Steve Robbins . . ." Michael Bach, *Birds of All Feathers: Doing Diversity and Inclusion Right* (Vancouver: Page Two Books, 2020) p. 11.

Page 127: "Research from 2017 by Deloitte found that 33 per cent of employees . . ." Inclusion pulse survey, https://www2.deloitte.com/content/dam/Deloitte/us/Documents/about-deloitte/us-about-deloitte-inclusion-survey.pdf

Page 127 "You can focus on the number of people . . ." Michael Bach, *Birds of All Feathers: Doing Diversity and Inclusion Right* (Vancouver: Page Two Books, 2020), p. 8.

Page 127: "A 2020 study by Glassdoor found diversity of a workplace . . ." Diversity & Inclusion Workplace Survey, https://www.glassdoor.com/employers/blog/diversity-inclusion-workplace-survey/

Page 128: "A study from Stanford University found that the praise women receive is different . . ." Therese Huston, "'He's like Tony Stark and she's like my mom': How workplace praise diverges between men and women," https://www.fastcompany.com/90594770/hes-like-tony-stark-and-shes-like-my-mom-how-workplace-praise-is-diverges-between-men-and-women

Page 132: "Michael Bach, the author of *Birds of All Feathers,* suggests beginning team meetings . . ." Michael Bach, *Birds of All Feathers: Doing Diversity and Inclusion Right* (Vancouver: Page Two Books, 2020) p. 84.

Bonus Section: At Least 101 More Staff Recognition Thoughts, Tips, Tools and Techniques

Page 167: "Employees who receive strong recognition will generate two times as many ideas per month . . ." "Complete Guide to Building Successful Employee Recognition Programs," https://www.octanner.com/uk/insights/articles/2019/4/3/employee_recognition_program_guide.html

Page 169: "A study by Emily Heaphy and Marcial Losada from Harvard University" Jack Zenger and Joseph Folkman, "The Ideal Praise-to-Criticism Ratio" https://hbr.org/2013/03/the-ideal-praise-to-criticism.

Page 172: "One of the questions The Gallup Organization asks . . ." Rodd Wagner and James K. Harter, *12: The Elements of Great Managing* (New York: Gallup Press, 2006) p. 49.

Acknowledgements

The first thing one discovers when writing a book is that it is not something you do on your own. It may "take a village to raise a child," but it takes almost as many helpers to launch a book.

First, I wish to acknowledge the many people who participated in programs at conferences and conventions and during on-site workshops over the past decade. Your comments, questions and feedback inspired me to write *Thanks, Again! More Simple, Inexpensive Ways for Busy Leaders to Recognize Staff.*

Throughout the writing process, I invited subscribers to my newsletter and people I know personally and professionally to read the manuscript, or parts of it. Lyle Karasiuk, Li Sin Wa (Wallis), Janice Lopez, Anita Wong, Tina Varagues, Aesha Tahir and Hussein Haymour all provided valuable feedback. Thanks again for sharing your insights so willingly. You contributed to making *Thanks, Again!* a better book.

Andrew Johnstone is the brilliant graphic designer with whom I have worked for nearly three decades. I marvel at how he can understand my often confused requests and create results far better than anything that I could have imagined. Andrew did such a splendid job of designing the cover for *Thanks, Again!* in a manner that links this book to my previous book, *Thanks! GREAT Job!* Andrew, thanks again for always making my writing look appealing.

Thanks also to our granddaughter, Paige Luck, for the author portrait on the back cover. She has just completed a two-year photographic technology program and launched her career as a professional photographer. I was happy to be one of her first customers (paigeluckphotography.com).

I would be remiss if I failed to acknowledge the patience and support of two women who I have never met in person but have spent hours with on the telephone and through emails. Publishing specialists Leanne Janzen and Dahlia Bellamy never exhibited frustration with my endless questions, requests and procrastination. I appreciate all the details they and the team behind them at FriesenPress wrangled to get this book into your hands. Leanne, thank you, and Dahlia, thank you, too!

And of course, there is Helen Metella. After more than 10 years, Helen has become more than the editor for my blog and my books. She has been an advisor who has kept me from publishing views that have no place in articles about staff recognition. She has warned me when my age was showing and suggested how to make my writing appeal to more contemporary audiences. She has been a muse, sharing stories which became the starting points for articles. Thanks, again, Helen, for covering so much ground.

Finally, there is my wife, June, who understands, or at least accepts, my need to keep writing. It's an addiction which so often becomes a barrier to completing all the tasks around the house that should receive my attention. (Yes dear, now that this book I done I'll get around to cleaning out the garage and the basement … maybe.) Thanks, again, June, for all your support and for sticking with me for more than half a century.

Conversation Starters for Book Clubs and Staff Recognition Mastermind Groups

1. *Thanks, Again!* was written for frontline leaders who "already believe in the power of staff recognition." Choosing to read the book makes you a "believer." How did you come to understand the power of staff recognition? Why is staff recognition important to you?
2. What research have you encountered that you see as evidence that staff recognition is important?
3. In Theme #1: Recognition Builds Workplace Relationships (p. 3), the author writes about the importance of caring, fairness, respect and trust in creating a workplace where people feel they belong and want to stay. How do you see staff recognition as a tool to create a positive workplace culture?
4. What are your most successful staff recognition practices? How do you assess the effectiveness of these practices?
5. Gallup found that the number one reason people leave organizations is a lack of recognition. Have you ever left a job because you didn't feel appreciated? Do you know someone else who quit because of a lack of recognition?
6. *Thanks, Again!* begins with Tip #1: The 4 As of Staff Recognition (p. xi)—"Not all staff recognition tips are created equally. Some will work for you. Other won't. There will be some that could be modified to fit your circumstances." You should **Adopt** tips that fit your workplace, **Adapt** others to fit and **Avoid** those that don't resonate with you.
    - Which staff recognition tips from *Thanks, Again!*, or from other sources, have you **Adopted** and which have you been able to **Adapt** to fit your workplace?

- Which ideas did you decide to **Avoid** because you felt they would not work for you and your staff?
- Describe a staff recognition technique that once worked in your workplace but which you recently decided to **Abandon** (or one that you feel you *should* **Abandon**). How did/do you know the technique has become stale or no longer works? How did you go about (or could you go about) retiring this staff recognition practice?

7. Theme #2: Filling Your Staff Recognition Tool Kit (p. 8) lists items to include in a staff recognition tool kit. What would you add to the list? Which items from the author's list would you exclude?

8. One of the questions Gallup asks to assess employee engagement is, "In the last seven days, have you received recognition or praise for good work?" How would your staff answer? How realistic is it to have a goal to recognize each staff member at least once a week?

9. An article in the *Harvard Business Review* in 2014 suggested that the ideal praise-to-criticism ratio was 5.6:1. What are your thoughts about this ratio and whether it is achievable?

10. Have you surveyed staff to determine how they feel about the recognition they receive? What questions did you ask? What did you discover that staff feel about the recognition within your organization? How have you used what you learned? How could you?

11. Have you conducted stay interviews (described in Theme #8: Building Commitment from Day One (p. 49)? What did you ask (or what would you ask)? What did you learn? How were you able to use this information?

12. Some people suggest that we can learn how to recognize staff by observing managers or supervisors who do a poor job of it or who never recognize anyone. What is your reaction to this statement?

13. The acronym **GREAT** (Theme #3: GREAT Staff Recognition: 5 Pieces that Make the Picture of Appreciation and Gratitude Complete (p. 12) is a reminder that meaningful staff recognition consists of five ingredients. Primarily, it must be **Genuine.** The message of appreciation becomes stronger as other ingredients

are added to make recognition **Relevant, Explicit, Appropriate and Timely**.
- What do you do to ensure the recognition you provide is **Genuine**?
- How have you been able to make staff recognition **Relevant** by linking it to your organization's core values and goals?
- How have you used a specific description of what the recipient did to make recognition **Explicit**?
- How have you used what you know about individual's interests and recognition preferences to provide recognition that is **Appropriate**?
- What strategies do you use to ensure that staff recognition is **Timely**?

14. What have you done (or could you do) to learn more about how staff members prefer to be recognized?
15. In *Thanks, Again!* the author addresses several reasons that managers give for not recognizing staff (Theme #27: How to Respond the Next Time Someone Says, "I Don't Recognize Staff Because . . ." (p. 150). Have you heard any of these excuses? What are your thoughts about the suggested responses?
16. *Thanks, Again!* includes suggestions on what you can do to make staff recognition a habit (Theme #5: Making Staff Recognition a Habit (p. 33). Which of these suggestions would work for you? What approaches have you used to develop good habits? How could these help you develop staff recognition habit?
17. Theme #6: Staff Recognition's Number One Tool: Thank-You Notes (p. 39)—How have recipients responded to your handwritten thank-you notes?
18. Which techniques from Theme #8: Building Commitment from Day One (p. 45) do you employ when people join your team? What else could you do to improve the chances that new staff members will feel that they are where they belong and will commit to staying with your organization?

19. Theme #10: Linking Staff Recognition to Career Goals (p. 59)—How have you linked the ways you recognize staff to their career goals?
20. Theme #11: Mine Customer Feedback for Reasons to Recognize Staff (p. 64)—How have you been able to use information from customers or clients to find reasons to recognize staff? What do you do (or could you do) to discover how customers feel about their encounters with your staff?
21. Which of the suggestions in Theme #13: Including Family Members in Your Staff Recognition Plans (p. 71) do you feel could work for you? Do you have other ways to involve family members in your staff recognition plans?
22. One way to recognize staff is with an activity that they can enjoy with their family. What family-friendly activities do you have or could you add to your staff recognition repertoire?
23. Theme #14: Important? Certainly. But Recognition Can Be Fun, Too (p. 75)—What are some fun ways that you have used to recognize staff?
24. Theme #15: A Year's Worth of Staff Recognition (p. 82)—Staff recognition knows no season and should never be limited to specific dates on the calendar, but there are some staff recognition practices that fit a specific time of the year more than other times. What are some examples of season-specific staff recognition?
25. Every year, there are hundreds of designated weeks and months and hundreds of designated days, some of which could be a catalyst for staff recognition. Which are some you could incorporate into your staff recognition plans?
26. Theme #16: Add Meaning to Formal Recognition (p. 95)—The author seems skeptical about the value of formal staff recognition programs. Based on your experience with formal recognition, what are your thoughts about the value of formal staff recognition programs?
27. Theme #18: Staff Recognition Goes Green (p. 102)—The author asks, "Are your staff recognition practices environmentally

friendly?" What is your answer? How could you "green up" your staff recognition?

28. Theme #20: Recognition by Everyone: Unleashing the Power of Peer Recognition (p. 113)—How have you encouraged peer recognition? What results have you had?

29. Theme #21: Recognition for Staff Who Work Remotely (p. 121)—How can we ensure that staff who never or seldom come into the office receive recognition that is as robust as that offered to onsite staff?

30. Theme #22: Diverse and Inclusive: Recognition for Workplaces Where Everyone Feels They Belong (p. 126)—What challenges to how you recognize staff has the diverse workplace created? How can these challenges be overcome? What have you done to ensure that how you recognize staff is inclusive?

31. Theme #25: A Penny-Pincher's Guide to Staff Recognition (p. 145)—The author suggests ways to recognize the contributions of staff within the constraints of limited budgets. What money-saving tips would you add to the list?

32. Theme #26: Staff Recognition Time Savers (p. 148)—Time is a precious resource. The author suggests several ways to make time to recognize staff. Which of these would work for you? What did the author leave out?

33. Of the thirty themes, which resonate with you the most? Which made the greatest impression on you? Why?

34. How did *Thanks, Again!* change how you think about staff recognition? Or how did it confirm what you already believed about staff recognition?

Want more Nelson?

Visit www.GREATstaffrecognition.com, where you can sign up for his biweekly newsletter, *Briefly Noted*, purchase a copy of his first book, *Thanks! GREAT Job!* and find other staff recognition resources.

Follow him on Twitter (https://twitter.com/nelsonscott_) or connect with him on LinkedIn (https://www.linkedin.com/in/nelson-scott-bbaa4711/).

Schedule him to present a keynote or breakout program at an upcoming convention or conference, or invite him to train members of your leadership team to hire, engage and retain the *right* people.

Phone: (780) 232-3828

Email: nmscott@telus.net

Printed in Canada